The Magnificent Natural Heritage of

South Africa

Johann Knobel

For my mother, my sisters,

and my late father.

Foreword

I am often asked what I consider to be the greatest challenge facing conservationists in South Africa today. For me there is one very clear imperative: we have to tell people about the natural wealth of our small corner of the earth and, even more importantly, to convince them that our collective prosperity is rooted in the care and wise use of these priceless wonders. It is no easy task in the face of emotionally and politically charged issues such as population growth, the short-term needs of people and their demands on land use.

ACKNOWLEDGEMENTS

Many people helped with this book, and I am deeply indebted to them.

George Bredenkamp kindly agreed to be the scientific editor, and brought together a formidable team of collaborating authors. To this day, I have not even met them all in person, but they all contributed their talents and expertise with a generosity not often experienced. I have been overwhelmed by their enthusiasm and unselfishness. They were kind and patient whenever I harassed them. My indebtedness to them cannot be adequately expressed.

My journey to find a publisher was a faith-testing one. Only after I had grown weary and discouraged did I meet a man with a vision similar to my own, Dick Wilkins of Sunbird Publishing, who immortalised my dream.

Mandy McKay did a marvellous job of the layout and design. Photographers are visual artists and are easily offended if designers do terrible things to their images. I am glad to say that I was elated with the wonderful things Mandy did with my photos. Her cover design, in particular, is to me a masterpiece of elegant simplicity and impact.

Brenda Brickman, working against 'scary deadlines' – to quote her own words – edited the writings of 13 different authors. I received numerous e-mail messages from Brenda late at night and over weekends, betraying the impossible hours she had been working. She cheerfully survived the schedule, politely bullied the sometimes grumpy photographer-compiler and the contributing authors (who tended to run off to places like the Kruger Park, Richtersveld, Baviaanskloof and even Europe at critical times) and pulled off everything in time – a sterling job.

Anton Boshoff's excellent underwater photographs added a much-needed extra dimension to the chapter on the coastline. Paul Brink, Coert Geldenhuys and Mark Skinner also contributed outstanding photographic material to fill the gaps in my own photography.

Deon Marais of the Department of Environmental Affairs and Tourism expertly prepared a biome map at a time of tremendous work pressure.

Ronald Lewis of Elardus Park processed my transparency films with pride and care, always combined with his refreshing sense of humour.

Brian Schwartz and Jan Pretorius of Foto Distributors assisted me in the acquisition of Nikon photographic equipment.

Many other dear friends helped by simply accompanying me on my journeys, offering me hospitality far from home, and in other ways too diverse to enumerate. I am sure they all know who they are, but I doubt whether they realise the extent to which they have enriched my life.

Finally, on the very deepest personal level, I would like to record my inestimable indebtedness to my mother, my sisters and my late father for their love and encouragement over the years.

And to the Creator of all things, my deepest gratitude – for everything.

Johann Knobel

SUNBIRD
PUBLISHING

Registration number: 4850177827

First published 1999 by Sunbird Publishing (Pty) Ltd, 34 Sunset Avenue, Llandudno, South Africa

Copyright © text Individual authors
Copyright © photography Johann C Knobel, with the exception of the following pages:
back cover (bottom right), pp 143, 146 (Anton Boshoff); pp 104 (bottom), 152 (bottom) (Paul Brink);
pg 124 (right) (Coert Geldenhuys); pg 30 (box) (GPL du Plessis [Photo Access]); 129, 136 (Mark Skinner)
Copyright © map Department of Environmental Affairs and Tourism
Copyright © published edition Sunbird Publishing

2 4 6 8 10 9 7 5 3 1

Publisher Dick Wilkins
Scientific editor George J Bredenkamp
Editor Brenda Brickman
Designer Mandy McKay
Production manager Andrew de Kock

Reproduction by Unifoto (Pty) Ltd, Cape Town
Printed and bound by Tien Wah Press (Pte) Ltd, Singapore

ISBN 0-62403-795-9

I journeyed to the wild places of South Africa.

I walked over naked sand dunes under a blazing sun. I wandered through forests dripping with cool moisture.
I waded barefoot through warm estuaries. I climbed to a mountain plateau 3 000 metres above sea level,
where melting snow penetrated my boots. I steered my car along a narrow track twisting among gigantic
trees lining a crocodile-infested river. I navigated unnerving mountain passes, past the rusted wrecks of
cars that had crashed into valleys below. I sped along arrow-straight tar roads across shimmering plains.

And everywhere I made discoveries.

I saw eagles fly. I saw lionesses explode from cover to crush the life out of a hapless antelope. I saw
jewel-like kingfishers mate above a sparkling pool. I saw delicate flowers opening to a semidesert sun.
I listened to legions of frogs clicking and chiming from moonlit reedbeds.
I smelled moist earth after a thunderstorm. I tasted cold, crisp water from gushing streams.

And my cameras worked overtime.

At first I was unaware of the fact that South Africa is arguably the botanical showpiece of the planet. I had to
learn that plants, more than anything else, qualify this country as one of the biodiversity giants of the world.
There are six floral kingdoms on earth, and only one of them is housed in its entirety within the political
boundaries of one country. That floral kingdom is the Cape Floristic Region, and the country is South Africa.

Thus enlightened, I had to return to the wilds – to focus my lenses on the plants. And my discoveries
were multiplied and my journeys were further enriched. I realised I had found one of the keys to the
uniqueness of South Africa's natural heritage.

And the plants also showed me the way to the biomes of South Africa ...

Contents

The Biomes of South Africa

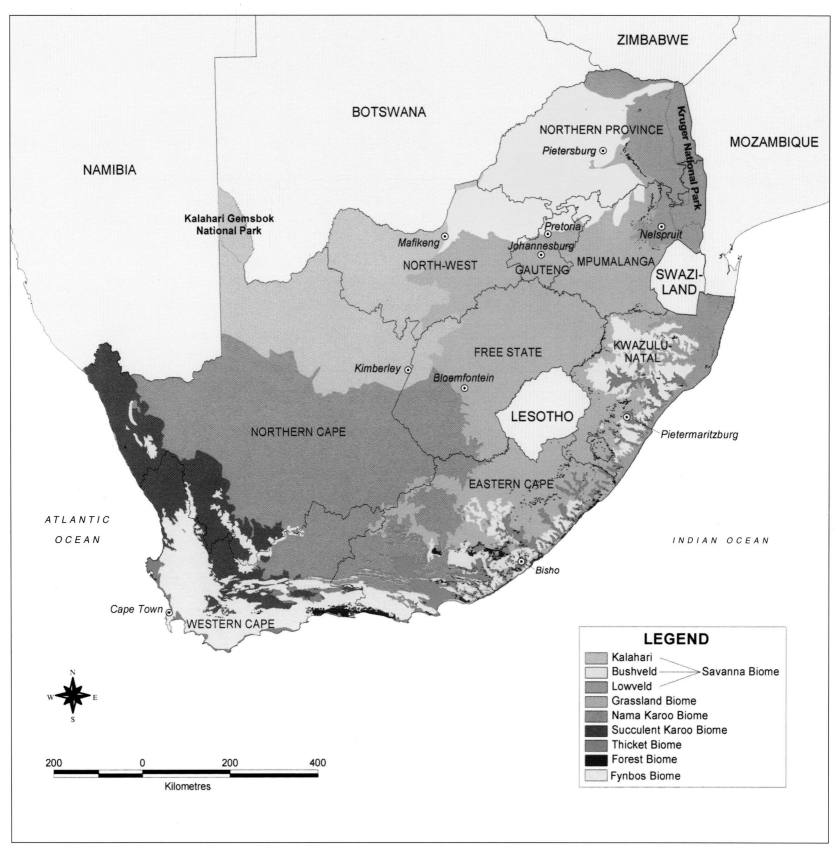

SOURCE: Vegetation of South Africa, Lesotho and Swaziland. Low, BA and Rebelo, AG (Eds). Department of Environmental Affairs and Tourism, Pretoria

Introduction

Johann Knobel

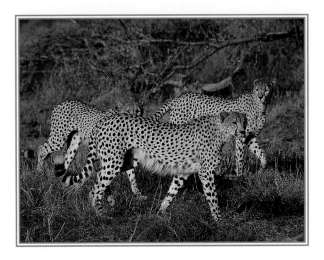

The chapters of this book have been based on the biomes of South Africa. Biomes are large ecological communities – or, if you like, ecosystems on a grand scale. South Africa is endowed with seven of these communities, each of which supports a unique diversity of plants and wildlife.

To identify the biomes, we must note the different growth forms of the plants that dominate the landscape. Three particular forms are important in this regard: trees and large shrubs that carry their growth buds higher than 0.7 metres above the ground; dwarf shrubs that carry their growth buds below 0.7 metres above the ground; and grasses and herbs that carry their growth buds at (or very close to) ground level.

We begin our journey through South Africa's magnificent natural heritage, in the northernmost and largest biome, the savanna. Savanna is dominated by a combination of trees and large shrubs, and grasses. This biome covers parts of the Northern Cape, North-West, Gauteng, most of the Northern Province, and parts of Mpumalanga, KwaZulu-Natal, and the Eastern Cape. It further extends north of the South African border across Namibia, Botswana, Zimbabwe, Mozambique, and indeed across much of the African continent. Because the savanna biome is so vast and rich in photographic potential, we have subdivided it into three parts for the purposes of this book: Kalahari, bushveld and lowveld.

South of the savanna biome, most of the interior of South Africa is occupied by two large biomes: grassland, and Nama karoo.

The grassland biome, dominated solely by grasses, covers most of the Free State, parts of North-West, most of Gauteng, parts of Mpumalanga, a small part of the Northern Province, and parts of KwaZulu-Natal and the Eastern Cape. The transition between the grassland and the Nama karoo biome is so gradual that it is almost impossible, when driving, to tell exactly what point you have left the one biome and entered the other.

Once you are well into the Nama karoo, however, it is easily recognised by a combination of dwarf shrubs and grasses (although the grasses may be either locally depleted or inconspicuous as a result of overgrazing and poor veld management). Nama karoo vegetation is not confined to the region known as the Great Karoo, but also covers parts of the Western Cape, Free State and much of the Northern Cape. It stretches beyond the borders into Namibia.

To the west of the Nama karoo is the succulent karoo biome, which is dominated exclusively by dwarf shrubs. It stretches along the western coastal plain of South Africa, and includes the regions known as Namaqualand and the Richtersveld, and to the southeast includes parts of the region known as the Little Karoo. It too extends north of the South African border, into Namibia.

South of the succulent karoo and Nama karoo biomes, the vegetation is dominated by a combination of dwarf shrubs, larger shrubs and trees, and, although true grasses are rare in this region, grass-like restios are abundant. This is the fynbos biome – part of the richest floral kingdom in the world. Fynbos vegetation is mainly restricted to a narrow coastal strip and the mountain ranges of the Western Cape, and parts of the Eastern and Northern Cape provinces.

In South Africa, forest and thicket constitute highly fragmented communities, occurring as isolated patches within the larger biomes. The forest biome consists of small pockets of vegetation dominated solely by trees and large shrubs. Forest patches occur – scattered amongst fynbos, grassland and savanna biomes – in the Northern Province, Mpumalanga, KwaZulu-Natal, the Eastern and Western Cape. In the deep river valleys of KwaZulu-Natal, and more extensively in the Eastern Cape, and in parts of the interior and the coastline of the Western Cape, landscapes are dominated by trees and large shrubs, in combination with dwarf shrubs. Scientists have only in recent times recognised this as a separate and distinct biome that is now referred to as the thicket biome.

These, then, are the biomes of South Africa.

However, we have also included chapters on three natural features of South Africa that are not biomes, but are nevertheless significant enough to merit special mention. These are the Great Escarpment, rivers and wetlands, and the coastline.

Kalahari

Noel van Rooyen

The Kalahari is one of Africa's last wilderness areas. It brings to mind images of camel thorn trees, sand dunes and valleys, beautiful sunsets, herds of antelope and large carnivores, and a climate of scorching summers and bitterly cold winter nights. Although commonly referred to as the 'Kalahari Desert', this remote area in the North-West and the far north of the Northern Cape (which includes the Kalahari Gemsbok National Park), continuing into Botswana, is not a true desert. Although rainfall is low in some areas, and large areas are covered by deep, loose sand, it does not approach the extreme aridity of true deserts. In fact, the Kalahari is densely covered with grasses, shrubs and trees.

Rain is the driving force behind the Kalahari ecosystem, and plants and animals respond dramatically to it when it arrives. The Kalahari's inaccessibility and the lack of surface water for most of the year have lessened the impact of man and contributed to the preservation of the area.

The name Kalahari originates from the Kgalagadi people who inhabit central Botswana. The word has many interpretations: it can mean 'wilderness', 'the land that has dried up', or 'salt pans'.

VEGETATION TYPES

Within the extensive Kalahari savanna system, seven major vegetation types have been described.

Thorny Kalahari dune bushveld

Thorny Kalahari dune bushveld is found on the deep sand in the Kalahari Gemsbok National Park at an altitude of approximately 1 000 metres.

The area is characterised by parallel dunes with dune 'streets', or valleys, and the vegetation consists of sparsely scattered trees – mainly camel thorn (*Acacia erioloba*), false umbrella thorn (*Acacia luederitzii*) and shepherd's tree (*Boscia albitrunca*).

Conspicuous grasses that are found within the thorny Kalahari dune bushveld include Lehmann's lovegrass (*Eragrostis lehmanniana*), Kalahari sour grass (*Schmidtia kalihariensis*) and Kalahari coach (*Stipagrostis amabilis*).

ABOVE A solitary gemsbok stands crisply defined against a backdrop of Kalahari grasses.

OPPOSITE Enormous sociable weaver nests are striking features of the Kalahari. A colony of up to 300 weavers may inhabit a single nest.

Shrubby Kalahari dune bushveld

The shrubby Kalahari dune bushveld covers most of the Kalahari Gemsbok National Park and the Gordonia district, and comprises gently undulating dunes, with pans scattered throughout this vegetation type. The vegetation is characterised by scattered shrubs of grey camel thorn (*Acacia haematoxylon*) and grasses such as *Stipagrostis amabilis*, ghagrass (*Centropodia glauca*) and giant three awn (*Aristida meridionalis*).

Karroid Kalahari bushveld

This vegetation type is found on flat, gravelly plains north of the Orange River. The tree layer in the karroid Kalahari bushveld is almost non-existent. Common shrubs are cauliflowerbush (*Salsola tuberculata*), kapokbos (*Eriocephalus ericoides*), and threethorn (*Rhigozum trichotomum*). Bushman grasses (*Stipagrostis ciliata* and *S. obtusa*) also occur.

Kalahari plains thorn bushveld

The Kalahari plains thorn bushveld is found on deep, loose sand in the eastern Kalahari, south of the Molopo River on undulating to flat plains. The area is characterised by a fairly good tree stratum with camel thorn and shepherd's tree as dominant trees, while black thorn (*Acacia mellifera*) and wild raisin (*Grewia flava*) dominate the shrub layer.

Kalahari mountain bushveld

Found on rocky, shallow soils on the hills in the southeastern Kalahari, the mountain bushveld vegetation is dominated by the camphor tree (*Tarchonanthus camphoratus*), lavender fever-berry (*Croton gratissimus*), and karoo kuni-bush (*Rhus burchellii*). Individuals of the wild olive (*Olea europaea* subsp. *africana*) are widely scattered in this vegetation type.

Kimberley thorn bushveld

The Kimberley thorn bushveld is an open savanna found in the Kimberley area. Umbrella thorn (*Acacia tortilis*) and camel thorn are the dominant tree species. Grasses such as red grass (*Themeda triandra*) and Lehmann's lovegrass are conspicuous.

Kalahari plateau bushveld

This vegetation type is confined to the Ghaap plateau in the Vryburg-Griekwastad area. It occurs on a sandy plateau, which is underlain by dolomite with calcrete deposits. The Kalahari plateau bushveld is a fairly dense bushveld composed of shrubs in a mixed grassland. The camphor tree, puzzle bush (*Ehretia rigida*) and wild raisin are dominant shrubs.

GEOLOGY AND SOILS

Geologically, the area covered by Kalahari sands extends over some 2.5 million square kilometres of the interior of central and southern Africa. These wind-blown sands constitute the largest continuous stretch of sand in the world. The present sand cover is thought to have developed about 19 000 to 16 000 years ago. It begins north of the Orange River, embraces the western two-thirds of Botswana, more than a third of Namibia, and stretches north through eastern Angola, western Zimbabwe and Zambia to southwestern Zaire and parts of the Democratic Republic of Congo at the equator. Rainfall decreases from north to south, ranging from a highly regular average rainfall of 1 000 millimetres a year in Zaire to an erratic and meagre 150 millimetres in the Northern Cape Province of South Africa.

The sands of the southern Kalahari display two reasonably distinct surfaces. In the extreme west and southwest, the sands are piled into a belt of dunes 800 kilometres long and 100 to 200 kilometres wide, while from just east of the dry Nossob riverbed the dunes are absent and the country is flat or slightly undulating. About 1 000 or more pans are scattered throughout the dune area and are focal points for many wildlife species.

Based on the size of the grains, two soil types occur in the Kalahari – coarser, sandy soils, and finer, more clay-like soils. The coarser soils occur widely, while the finer soils are generally confined to riverbeds and pans. These soils display an interesting difference in water holding capacity – the so-called 'inverse texture effect'. In arid regions the coarser, sandy soils generally hold moisture better than finer soils because of lower run-off and better infiltration of rainwater. Poor capillary forces reduce upward movement of soil water and evaporation is restricted to the soil surface. In contrast, the fine-textured soils have a higher clay content, poor infiltration, higher run-off and high evaporation rates. However, the high mineral and nutrient concentrations

CONSERVATION

Conservation within and of the savanna biome is good in principle, mainly due to the presence of a number of wildlife reserves. Urbanisation is not a threat, perhaps because the hot, dry climate and diseases prominent in the savanna areas have hindered urban development. Much of the area too is used for game farming, and the importance of tourism and big-game hunting in the conservation area must not be underestimated.

Savannas are the basis of the African wildlife and ecotourism industry, and play a major role in the meat industry.

ABOVE A young giraffe lies up among the bushveld grasses.

SAVANNA – THE AFRICAN PARADOX

The savanna biome is the largest biome in southern Africa, and covers about 46 per cent of its area.

Savanna is well developed in South Africa, and covers the north-central and northeastern reaches of the country, stretching southwards along the western edge of the grassland biome, following much of the coastline of KwaZulu-Natal, and even extending into parts of the Eastern Cape. It is also the dominant vegetation of Botswana, Namibia and Zimbabwe.

The term savanna is widely accepted as describing a vegetation type with a well-developed grassy layer and an upper layer of woody plants.

In this large area, many environmental factors correlate with the distribution of different savanna vegetation types. These include landform, climate, soil types, fire and a very specific fauna. South African savannas of nutrient-poor substrates are characteristically broad-leaved and without thorns, while those of nutrient-rich substrates are fine-leaved and thorny. Nutrient-rich savannas have a high grass layer productivity and the grasses are acceptable to grazers, resulting in a high grazing capacity. Both types may occur close to each other on a single farm or small nature reserve.

Because the savanna biome is so vast, and to accommodate all the photographic and textual material we have collected, we have split this biome into three sections: the Kalahari savanna is a sandy, arid region in the western interior; what we have referred to as the bushveld is the central, moister area east of the Kalahari savanna but west of the Escarpment, and includes savanna regions in the Eastern Cape and at middle and higher altitudes in KwaZulu-Natal; while the lowland areas east of the Escarpment are what is known as the Lowveld.

Although the principal elements of savanna are trees and grasses, the ecology of this vegetation is neither that of grassland, nor that of forest. The complex interactions between trees and grasses give this vegetation a character of its own, easily recognisable as a distinct biome.

BIODIVERSITY AND ENDEMISM

The African savanna has 13 000 plant species, of which 8 000 are savanna endemics. In South Africa, moist savannas have more than 3 800 plant species, and dry savannas more than 3 300. This plant biodiversity equals that of the South African grasslands, and is only exceeded by the fynbos biome.

In respect of animal biodiversity, the savannas are without peer. South African savannas have more recorded species of amphibians (57 in moist and 52 in dry savannas); reptiles (162 in moist and 177 in dry savannas); birds (540 in moist and 519 in dry savannas) and mammals (153 in moist and 171 in dry savannas), than any other biome. About 50 per cent of the plants of the savannas occur in nature reserves, while more than 90 per cent of the vertebrate savanna animals have been reported to occur in nature reserves.

ABOVE This is arguably the most typical face of Africa: grass and flat-topped trees. The principle elements of a savanna are trees and grasses, but the ecology of a savanna is neither that of a grassland, nor that of a forest.

Altitudes within the savanna biome are erratic, and can range from 2 000 metres to sea level. Rainfall varies from 200 to 1 000 millimetres a year, and almost every major geological and soil type occurs within the biome.

A major delimitating factor of the biome as a whole is the lack of rainfall sufficient to permit the upper woody plant layer to dominate, and this, coupled with important ecological factors such as fire and grazing, ensures a dominant grass layer.

However, most savanna species – both grass and tree – are adapted to survive fires, and less than 10 per cent are destroyed by it. Even with severe burning, most species can resprout from the stem bases.

Most savanna vegetation types are conducive to grazing, by cattle or game. However, in the short term, grazing too may affect the ratio of woody versus grass species cover, as overgrazing often enhances the development of a woody component in transitional areas between typical bushveld and grassland areas.

In savanna, wet seasons tend to be hot, and dry seasons warm. The lack of low temperatures, even during the somewhat cooler dry season, favours the tropical character of savannas.

Evaporation is higher than rainfall, so savannas have a water deficit for most of the year.

ABOVE Two gemsbok battle it out with their rapier-like horns.

ABOVE A brown hyena drinks at a waterhole early in the morning.

of the fine riverine and pan soils result in a more palatable vegetation. Vegetation on the nutrient-deficient dune sands has relatively easier access to water, but is of a poorer quality.

KALAHARI GEMSBOK NATIONAL PARK

The Kalahari Gemsbok National Park is situated in the duneveld area, while its sister reserve, the Gemsbok National Park in Botswana, consists mostly of flat to undulating country. Together these two parks form a vast international conservation area called the Kgalagadi Transfrontier Park (see box on page 20), straddling about 250 kilometres of the South Africa/Botswana border. The border between the Kalahari Gemsbok National Park and the Gemsbok National Park is unfenced, and is a pragmatic recognition that wildlife is contained not by political boundaries but by physical barriers.

The Kalahari Gemsbok National Park was established in 1931 and forms a triangle that covers some 9 593 square kilometres between the fenced Namibian border to the west, and the ancient Auob and Nossob rivers. The area just south of the Auob River was fenced during the early sixties, and, together with the fence that was later erected north of the Molopo River, has effectively blocked the migratory route of springbok (*Antidorcas marsupialis*), blue wildebeest (*Connochaetes taurinus*) and eland (*Taurotragus oryx*) to the Orange River in the distant south. The altitude of the park varies from 870 metres at Twee Rivieren in the south, to 1 080 metres at Union's End in the north.

The largest portion of the Kalahari Gemsbok park lies in a region with long, reddish sand dunes that run in parallel rows from the northwest to the southeast, in places rising some 15 to 30 meters above the dune valleys or 'streets' between them.

The average annual rainfall ranges from 200 to 230 millimetres, although the rainfall can vary from less than 100 millimetres to more than 700 millimetres a year. Although rainfall is erratic, the highest precipitation occurs in the four months January to April, with a peak in March. Temperatures are extreme with winter lows falling to minus 11°C and summer highs reaching 45°C.

WATER, LIFEBLOOD OF THE KALAHARI

The river systems and pans of the Kalahari Gemsbok National Park are its most important physical asset, even though they usually contain no natural surface water. Although they only cover about four per cent of the total area of the park, they sustain most of the animal life in terms of palatable grazing, potable water and habitat diversity. They contribute to localised animal migration through a phenomenon of wet season concentrations of animals around the river, and dry season dispersion.

The timing and amount of seasonal rainfall, the existence of relatively long-term rainfall/drought cycles, and the occurrence of sporadic floods in the Auob and Nossob rivers apparently play a major role in the vegetation dynamics in the Kalahari.

The regeneration of the dominant woody species, the camel thorn and the grey camel thorn is possibly dependent on floods and/or consecutive years of average to above average rainfall. Droughts, grazing and fire have a negative effect on the establishment of *Acacia* seedlings. In 1934 the Nossob River flooded and the last flood that was recorded was in 1963, whereas the Auob River floods about once every 11 years.

The borehole controversy

Within the Kalahari Gemsbok National Park, borehole-fed watering points were created in the 1930s. The thinking behind their construction was to preserve the full spectrum of natural fauna, and to sustain migratory herds throughout the relatively long dry season. In addition, they were thought to bring about more effective utilisation of the

ABOVE A springbok 'pronks' by bouncing along on stiff legs.

available grazing, to prevent interference with farming by halting animal migrations to the south and west in search of food and water, and to utilise the tourist potential of the area. The usefulness and effect of this practice has been subject to much speculation and controversy. Arguments against the provision of water are that they interfere with a natural system, the alleged overgrazing and bush encroachment in the immediate vicinity of watering points, and the discouragement of animal migration. And, since many game species in the Kalahari are water independent, it has been suggested that artificial waterholes are not an essential source of water.

Recent studies in the Kalahari Gemsbok park have demonstrated that, although the vegetation and animal numbers of the combined conservation area (South Africa/Botswana) show definite changes in the short to medium term, an ecological balance exists at present and this balance should be sustained if the present large size of this conservation area is maintained. Although localised gradients in herbaceous plant species composition caused by grazing do occur in the different habitats, these are not related to the presence or effect of artificial water supplies.

It seems that the grazing/trampling effect around a waterhole is restricted to the immediate vicinity of the waterhole, and no definite gradient is discernable in the vegetation as distance from the watering point increases. Even the less water-dependent species such as gemsbok and red hartebeest, are attracted to the waterholes. These animals utilise the waterholes rather for the minerals (lick sites) than for the moisture. The same applies to pans in the Kalahari where natural licks, which are scarce in the surrounding sandy areas, are the main attraction for game.

Some of the possible consequences of uniformly spaced artificial watering points would be an increase in non-mobile, water-dependent game species. However, over decades the numbers of the different game species in the Kalahari Gemsbok park have fluctuated seasonally and

ABOVE A magnificent male lion is bathed in the golden glow of the dying sun. In the Kalahari, lions have to survive without water for long periods of time.

FROM LEFT TO RIGHT Most sociable weaver nests house a pair of pygmy falcons as uninvited guests. The pygmy falcon weighs only about 60 grams, and is smaller than a dove;
An impressive giant eagle owl waits for nightfall, when it will venture from its perch to hunt; A colourful agama lizard perches high in a threethorn shrub; A marico flycatcher
sits quietly on one of the lower branches of a camel thorn tree, from where it watches for insect prey.

SAVANNA RAPTORS

The African savanna supports a greater diversity of birds of prey than any other region on earth. These range in size from the massive Cape vulture (Gyps coprotheres) and lappet-faced vulture (Torgos tracheliotus) – the former having been recorded to weigh in at an impressive 10 kilograms – to the diminutive pygmy falcon (Polihierax semitorquatus) and African scops owl (Otus senegalensis), at about 60 grams each.

A wide spectrum of animals is taken by hunting raptors. Larger birds of prey, such as the martial eagle (Polemaetus bellicosus) and the crowned eagle (Stephanoaetus coronatus), are perfectly capable of killing small antelopes, young warthogs and monkeys, while other raptors feed on insects.

Some are specialist feeders: the black (or Verreaux's) eagle (Aquila verreauxii) favours dassies, snake eagles (Circaetus sp.) prefer snakes, while the African fish eagle (Haliaeetus vocifer), osprey (Pandion haliaetus) and Pel's fishing owl (Scotopelia peli) prefer fish. The bat hawk (Macheiramphus alcinus), as its name suggests, feeds on bats, and the honey buzzard (Pernis apivorus) prefers the larvae of bees and wasps.

Many birds of prey eat carrion. Some, like the tawny eagle (Aquila rapax), like to rob other avian hunters of their hard-won prey, and yellow-billed kites (Milvus migrans parasitus) are adept at stealing food from humans. Probably the strangest of all the raptors, the palm-nut vulture (Gypohierax angolensis) has, as its name suggests, a partially vegetarian diet!

JOHANN KNOBEL

a sustained eruption or increase in their numbers has never been evident, suggesting that there are other factors such as habitat, food quality and quantity limiting their numbers.

VEGETATION OF THE KALAHARI GEMSBOK

The Kalahari Gemsbok National Park sustains some 500 plant species. Dominant plant families are the grasses (Poaceae) (66 species), legumes (Fabaceae) (63 species), daisies (Asteraceae) (53 species), and lilies (Liliaceae). Genera with the highest number of species are *Eragrostis, Limeum, Hermannia, Indigofera* and *Dipcadi*. Dune crests are covered by what can best be described as a sea of grass – tall, thick duinriet (*Stipagrostis amabilis*), which binds the sand and stabilises the dunes.

The vegetation is dominated by grasses and ephemerals or annual plants. Although trees and shrubs contribute only eight per cent to the life form spectrum, they are visually dominant and confirm the marginal savanna character of the southern Kalahari. The high percentage of annual species (31 per cent) correlates more with desert areas. There are very few succulent species in this summer rainfall area, however, up to 21 per cent of the species are bulbous/semibulbous plants.

Large camel thorn trees are prominent in the dry beds of the Nossob, Auob, Molopo and Kuruman rivers, and small buffalo grass (*Panicum coloratum*) prevails in the fine alluvial soils of the riverbeds.

The river banks are dominated by threethorn and small bushman grass. The most common trees and shrubs that can be found on the sandy dunes and plains include the camel thorn, grey camel thorn and the shepherd's tree.

ABOVE After good summer rains, the Kalahari duneveld is transformed into a soft, undulating sea of green grasses.

Perennial plant species are the backbone of the system, providing many animals with a stable supply of food in both the wet and dry seasons. The annual species can be regarded as an unreliable luxury, abundant during favourable conditions but absent during droughts. They survive in the form of a dormant seed bank. However, annuals often have large, showy flowers that attract insects and give the desert short but spectacular splashes of colour.

Survival strategies

Seed dispersal at the end of the rainy season should be efficient and many seeds (for example, *Cynanchum orangeanum*) are dispersed by wind, ants (grasses and herb species), mammals (camel thorn, devil's claw – *Harpagophytum procumbens*, and burr bristlegrass – *Setaria verticillata*) and birds (raisin bush – *Grewia retinervis, and Lycium* spp.). Seeds of the bushman grasses (*Stipagrostis* spp.) are able to twist with a corkscrew action to penetrate into the sand. Bird dispersed plant species such as waxberry (*Pollichia campestris*),

Lycium bosciifolium, raisin bush, *Boscia albitrunca* and *Solanum capense* are present beneath all large trees.

Similarly, plants species with seeds dispersed on the hair (fur) of mammals, such as *Setaria verticillata* and *Tribulus zeyheri*, are also more abundant under large trees.

During the hot dry season (September to January) most woody species (perennials) are leafless to reduce water loss.

Grapple plant or devil's claw grows widespread on the Kalahari sands. Its dry fruit projects a number of short, hard and twisted protrusions that resemble vicious hooks and barbs. The fruit easily sticks to the hoof or foot of an animal, and the seeds are then very efficiently and widely dispersed.

The grasses, especially the annual species, are dry and crumbled. Annual bulbs and tubers survive beneath the ground while other species survive as dormant seeds in the soil seed bank. During this period plants without storage organs or with roots that do not penetrate deep into the sands wither away and die.

KGALAGADI TRANSFRONTIER PARK

In 1999, 51 years after wildlife authorities made an informal arrangement to cooperate, the presidents of Botswana and South Africa signed a treaty linking the Gemsbok National Park and the Kalahari Gemsbok National Park. The new park, covering an area of 37 991 square kilometres (almost twice the size of the Kruger National Park), is called the Kgalagadi Transfrontier Park (KTP). The treaty has set a precedent for all the other transfrontier projects in the region, and the park is regarded as a model of international cooperation in conservation.

Current land-claim negotiations are underway, and it seems likely that some of the Bushman [San] communities that live to the south of the KTP will have rights to gain access to, and even own part of the existing Kalahari Gemsbok National Park. International interest in the Bushmen is an important ecotourism factor, and integrating their culture into the park could well add considerable value to its meaningfulness.

The Peace Parks Foundation is dedicated to creating a vast network of transfrontier conservation areas in southern Africa, promoting regional cooperation, job creation and biodiversity conservation.

*Peace Parks Foundation review
(Africa – Environment & Wildlife, Vol.7 No.3)*

ABOVE A ground squirrel grooms a clan member. In the heat of the day, these squirrels use their bushy tails as parasols to shade themselves.

Perennial grasses such as Lehmann's lovegrass and the large and small bushman grasses (*Stipagrostis* spp.) remain dormant, with nutrients stored in their deeper, penetrating roots, but a few active green blades can usually still be found. The roots of the perennial grasses in the upper sand layer are equally affected by the hot, dry sand, and in response they have evolved a protective sand sheath around the roots.

Fire damage

Fires occur rarely, but lightning fires do occur, especially after years of above-average rainfall, when there is abundant vegetation to fuel them. At such times, large fires can sweep through the Kalahari and can burn down large camel thorn trees, such as happened in the Nossob River in the mid-seventies. Approximately 33 per cent of the trees died in this fire. The smaller grey camel thorn, however, showed a survival of 90 per cent after a fire in the grassy interior dune veld of the Kalahari Gemsbok National Park in 1992. This tree regrows from underground growth buds called adventituous buds, an adaptation of most savanna woody shrubs.

About 35 per cent of the area of the Kalahari Gemsbok National Park was burnt in 1994/95 and the mortality of woody species was, on average, less than 20 per cent.

WILDLIFE

The Kalahari Gemsbok National Park sustains a remarkable variety of wildlife, from the largest carnivores, to antelope and other mammals (60 species in total), through to an abundance of birds, insects, spiders, scorpions and other invertebrates.

Of the 55 species of reptiles found in the park, the remarkable barking gecko (*Ptenopus garrulus*) is probably the most audible. At dusk in summer, the males make a sound that is similar to that of hitting two pebbles together. The geckos' incessant chatter has kept many a visitor to the Kalahari awake for most of the night. The barking gecko is a nocturnal lizard that burrows in the sand.

More than 260 species of birds occur, including a rich diversity of raptors and other dry land 'specials', but perhaps the most obvious species is the sociable weaver (*Philetairus socius*), whose presence is easily told from its enormous communal nests that litter old *Acacia* trees throughout the region. The nests are made predominantly from grass, carefully laid in an interlocking pattern until the structure is completed. They are punctuated throughout with small tunnels that lead into the separate chambers of paired birds. Many hundreds of birds inhabit a single communal nest, and it provides an ideal refuge from excessive temperatures. The nests are warm, comfortable, waterproof and last for decades. Sometimes the nests are so large that their sheer weight, especially after a rainstorm, causes the branches to collapse and the nest to be thrown to the ground.

Sociable weavers do not normally drink and depend on termites as a major source of food.

Six cat species occur in the Kalahari: black-footed cat (*Felis nigripes*), African wild cat (*F. lybica*), caracal (*F. caracal*), cheetah (*Acinonyx jubatus*), leopard (*Panthera pardus*) and lion (*P. leo*).

The lion is the Kalahari's biggest predator and is widespread throughout the area. The more arid and open environment of the southern Kalahari impacts upon the distribution, diversity and density of prey species, and so Kalahari lions have to travel extraordinarily far to find and catch prey. Travel distances of more than 40 kilometres a night have been measured. These lions occupy loosely defined territories of up to 1 200 square kilometres because of the scarcity of prey and the distances involved in hunting. Small mammals and young animals make up more than 50 per cent of lion kills in the Kalahari, compared to less than one per cent in the Kruger National Park. Kalahari lions kill about 47 animals per year compared to about 15 animals a year in the Kruger. Their range of diet is wide and when larger prey species are scarce they will eat anything that comes their way, even ostrich eggs. Kalahari lions' meal preferences are, firstly, wildebeest, then gemsbok (*Oryx gazella*), springbok, and red hartebeest (*Alcelaphus buselaphus*), and then animals like porcupine (*Hystrix africaeaustralis*), ostriches (*Struthio camelus*) and aardvark (*Orycteropus afer*). Leopards are loners, and males and females have separate, although overlapping, hunting ranges or territories of about 400 square kilometres. Nocturnal hunters, leopards live by day in old aardvark holes, in dense shade under bushes, or in the cool crevices of the calcrete cliffs along the rivers. They also have to travel long distances in search of prey, and distances of more than 33 kilometres per night – with an average of 14 kilometres – have been recorded.

Cheetah, on the other hand, are more sociable, and hunt during the day. The Kalahari riverbeds – and the narrow Auob River in particular – are considered by some to be the best areas in Africa to watch a cheetah on the hunt. These dry courses concentrate prey species such as springbok into relatively confined, yet sparsely vegetated areas – ideal for observation.

ABOVE A small group of ostriches looks for food in the Nossob riverbed.

ABOVE A female cheetah and her cubs seek shade in the midday heat.

Food and water sources

To cope with the intense heat and scarcity of water, animals have had to evolve some remarkable adaptations in order to survive.

The ground squirrel (*Xerus inauris*) lives in extensive, multiholed burrows, but is a diurnal and sociable rodent. It has its own, built-in shade-provider – in the shape of a large bushy tail. The tail is flicked up and held in a gentle arc over the body while facing away from the sun.

The squirrel does not need to drink water, as it possess very efficient, water-absorbing kidneys, which means that its urine is highly concentrated and a minimum of water is lost.

The Namaqua (*Pterocles namaqua*) and Burchell's (*P. burchelli*) sandgrouses are seed-eaters and especially the young ones, therefore, need water for survival. The male bird physically carries water to the young by soaking his specially adapted belly feathers in water, and flying

BIODIVERSITY AND CONSERVATION IN THE KALAHARI GEMSBOK

Preliminary data on the age structure of the camel thorn trees in the upper Nossob River show a poor survival of seedlings and an almost complete absence of juvenile plants. If the regeneration of the camel thorn is dependent on flooding, the building of dams in the upper reaches of the Auob and Nossob rivers in Namibia, preventing flood waters from reaching the park, could have disastrous effects on the long-term ecology of the park. Biodiversity is regarded as a measure of richness of species in a faunal and/or floral region, and desert or semiarid areas such as the Kalahari are important in the global effort to conserve diversity, because they are fragile and vulnerable to the pernicious effects of environmental degradation.

The 500 plant species recorded in the Kalahari Gemsbok are much lower in comparison to the eastern mesic savanna areas. The average richness of 20 species per 100-square-metre sample plot is also low compared to the 40 to more than 50 species per sample plot recorded in more mesic savannas in the east. The Kalahari has the lowest species/area ratio of all the regions in southern Africa, and can floristically be regarded as relatively depauperate. There are also very few endemic species in the southern Kalahari and less than three per cent of the total number of plant species are estimated to be endemic to the area. The Kalahari is therefore not a 'hot spot' in terms of plant species richness or rarity, or endemism, probably as a result of fairly

recent sand deposits, low topographical diversity, low rainfall, large homogeneous sandy areas and the lack of discontinuities that create isolation.

Why then conserve the Kalahari? The very existence of the park proves that whereas high biodiversity is undoubtedly a compelling reason for conservation, it is by no means the only one. The Kalahari Gemsbok is the last part of South Africa where animals such as gemsbok, eland, blue wildebeest and springbok can still migrate or undertake nomadic movements across international boundaries. It is the last part of South Africa where large predators like lion, leopard, cheetah and hyena roam unencircled by human-made fences. It is also a refuge for countless birds of prey. Many of these creatures need large territories to survive, and therefore large land areas are needed to adequately conserve them. In South Africa, the Kalahari Gemsbok is the only arid park that currently fits the bill. It is a magnificent outdoor laboratory for scientists wishing to unravel the dynamics of arid savanna ecology. The South African park, in conjunction with the neighbouring conservation areas that make up the Kgalagadi Transfrontier Park (see box on page 20), is arguably the finest arid savanna reserve on earth. Even so, although almost 20 per cent of the Kalahari savanna is presently conserved, less than one per cent of the Kalahari mountain bushveld, Kalahari plains thorn bushveld, Kalahari plateau bushveld and the karroid Kalahari bushveld is conserved.

back to the nest (over distances of up to 60 kilometres), where the young drink from the saturated feathers. As much as 20 to 40 millilitres of water can be held in this way.

All the carnivores in the Kalahari Gemsbok National Park are independent of water, but the larger ones will utilise it if it is available. Lions in this area have to survive without water for long periods of time. Given an adequate kill rate, their water needs are surprisingly low. Lying in the shade of trees during the heat of day is a way of reducing evaporative water loss and of keeping their body temperatures low.

Gemsbok show remarkable heat tolerance by allowing their body temperature to rise during the day to avoid having to cool off by sweating. For the vital organs such as the brain to survive body temperatures of up to 45°C the gemsbok has developed an extraordinary heat exchange unit, known as carotid rete, in the large sinus region below the brain. The carotid rete system cools the hot arterial blood from the body before it enters the brain. This permits the animal's body temperature to rise while the temperature of the heat-sensitive brain remains well below lethal levels. Many other antelope species can reduce water loss by slowing their metabolic rate and therefore reducing faecal water loss, urinatory water loss and respiratory evaporation. However, even herbivores differ from one another in their ability to survive in the waterless Kalahari, and these differences were evidenced during the serious drought that occurred in the mid-eighties. The order in which the different antelope species succumbed to the dry conditions reflected their different abilities to survive: blue wildebeest, eland, red hartebeest, gemsbok and springbok. Springbok owe their great success in the deserts to their their unusual ability to both browse and graze.

Plants and animals alike are under stress during the early summer months, conserving their water reserves as best they can. Grass moisture content drops to below two per cent in October, too low to satisfy the water demands of grazing ungulates. Animals have to resort to other sources of water such as tsamma melons (*Citrullus lanatus*).

Also, during the cooler nights the water content of plants increases, so grazing animals can increase their water intake.

This probably explains why gemsbok and blue wildebeest spend a lot of time feeding at night.

The aesthetically pleasing *Acacia* tree component of the park is well developed within the river system and provides indispensable micro-habitats for wildlife in the harsh climatic conditions. The big, rough-barked, thick-stemmed camel thorn is the most common large tree in the Kalahari, and some specimens grow up to 15 metres in height. Its components and facilities are utilised by man, browsers, carnivores, rodents, snakes, insects, lizards, skinks, scorpions, tampans and birds.

Large trees scattered throughout the southern Kalahari are focal points for animal activity. Mammals frequently stand underneath tree

ABOVE Plover tracks on the Witsand – white sand – near Postmasburg.

ABOVE A female bateleur sweeps gracefully through the sky.

canopies during the heat of day and their dung is concentrated in these areas. Big trees are used as nest and roost sites by a great variety of bird species, especially the sociable weaver, secretary bird (*Sagittarius serpentarius*), bateleur (*Terathopius ecaudatus*) and martial eagle (*Polemaetus bellicosus*). Over decades fallen nest material and the faeces of birds and mammals has enriched the soil beneath large trees. The nitrogen levels are 200 to 500 per cent and the phosphorus levels 150 to 250 per cent higher than the surrounding sandy plains.

The shepherd's tree plays an important ecological role in the Kalahari. This tree creates a cavern of cool shadow in a hot and often shadeless region. These shady places are often occupied by lion or leopard, as the temperature on the shaded sand surface can be as much as 20°C lower than the surrounding areas. The evergreen foliage is rich in moisture, vitamins and proteins. The leaves have medicinal value and the powdered root has preservative properties for butter and milk, is a fair substitute for coffee or chicory, and is used for porridge and for fermenting beer.

The response of the threethorn to rain is rapid, and within five days these shrubs produce flowers and a nutritious pod and leaves a week later. In late spring (October) its flowers and fruit can sometimes be the only fresh food for the smaller antelope such as springbok. They can be seen walking from shrub to shrub picking off the flowers and pods.

The small, round tsamma melon, initially green but fading to yellow at the end of the season, forms a very important substitute for drinking water, although its watery inside is rather tasteless. More than 90 per cent of the melon's content is water. Its occurrence and numbers in the dunes is very erratic and dependent upon the right amount of rainfall. Tsamma melons are a highly sought after source of food and water, and are utilised by insects, birds, rodents, mammals (including carnivores), and man. The melons are fairly frost resistant, and if buried in the sand they store very well and remain edible for more than a year. The nutritious seeds, crushed into a fine powder and mixed with water, make a tasteless but healthy porridge.

Wild cucumbers (*Cucumis africanus*), and greenish to yellow gemsbok cucumbers (*Acanthosicyos naudinianus*), are also consumed by animals. The fruits are covered with fine sharp spines that act, to a limited degree, as animal deterrents. After the first frost from May onwards, the cucumbers soften and decompose quickly. The enlarged tap root of the gemsbok cucumber penetrates 1.5 metres into the sand and is excavated and chewed by porcupine, steenbok (*Raphicerus campestris*), springbok, gemsbok, red hartebeest, and eland for its bitter, yet lifesaving moisture.

Dense stands of the sour-smelling Kalahari sour grass usually cover vast areas of the Kalahari after good summer rains. It is the first grass to recolonise barren areas after drought and/or areas disturbed by grazing and trampling. This grass provides fairly good fodder when just sprouting, or when dried out in late winter, but is highly unpalatable when mature and green. It exudes an irritating acidic substance that often causes skin irritation, eye infection and swelling of the tongue in both humans and ungulates.

The grapple plant's storage roots have medicinal properties, and are widely harvested and utilised in Namibia and Botswana.

Kalahari truffles (*Terfezia* sp.), resembling potatoes, are the fruiting body of a fungus and, growing beneath the ground during favourable seasons, they require a special skill to be found. Especially during April the surface of the sand in certain habitats should be inspected for telltale cracks from where the rather tasty and nutritious truffles can be removed for human consumption.

Symbiotic relationships

One of the less appealing of the Kalahari residents is an animal that has earned itself a most unwelcome reputation. The sand tampan (*Ornithodorus moubata*), or tampan tick, is a highly specialised creature in that it cannot tolerate exposure to sun or sand temperatures above 55°C. Because of this it has a flat body with long legs to facilitate movement through the sand. Its skin is covered with a waxy layer to protect it against dehydration. Tampans select a suitable shady site – for example,

ABOVE In the extreme southwest of the Kalahari, the sands are piled into an 800-kilometre-long and up to 200-kilometre-wide belt of dunes, usually stabilised by vegatation.

under the canopy of a camel thorn tree – and wait, buried in the sand, and in ambush, for a hot-blooded victim.

Vibrations caused by movement, and built-in carbon dioxide detectors, quickly help them to locate a host. They emerge in numbers, feed and fall back onto the sand when their prey shows signs of leaving the shaded area. Their saliva contains a mild neurotoxin that anaesthetises the bite area, making the host almost unaware of its presence.

A unique kind of symbiosis is encountered between honey badgers (*Mellivora capensis*), black-backed jackals (*Canis mesomelas*) and the pale chanting goshawk (*Melierax canorus*). Badgers frequently dig for small animals in the sand, and jackals and goshawks follow the badgers around to snap up those prey items that are quick enough to escape the badgers' depredations.

Most sociable weaver nests have a pair of pygmy falcons (*Polihierax semitorquatus*) as uninvited tenants. The falcons seldom catch the weavers, as their choice food is lizards. Their presence most probably assists the weavers by deterring other predators.

Pygmy falcons weigh only about 60 grams each, and are smaller than doves. In winter their small bodies and associated high metabolisms cannot resist cold exposure for long, and they practise huddling as a means to share each other's warmth and survive the cold nights. They use well-insulated woodpecker holes and sociable weaver nests to breed in, efficiently escaping the rigours of the outside Kalahari environment.

Migrations

There are several migration patterns within the greater Kalahari, but in the southwest where the Kalahari Gemsbok National Park lies, animals tend to move anticlockwise, travelling slowly and in a large, loose circle towards the northeast in the summer, and returning to the southwest in the winter. The Gemsbok National Park in Botswana consists of some dunes, but is mostly a fairly dense and flat savanna into which the animals move when rain produces greener pastures there.

Any barrier to the movement of animals across the Nossob River will be disastrous to the southern Kalahari ecosystem. Large migrations involving wildebeest, eland, springbok and sometimes red hartebeest from Botswana into the Kalahari Gemsbok National Park occurred during the years 1930, 1938, 1946, 1950, 1961, 1964, 1979, 1983, 1985 – all apparently during dry periods. The animals seemed to be either moving away from poor conditions, or towards more favourable ones.

When the land in the north is dry and bare, animals move towards the Auob and Nossob rivers, to which they have been coming since time immemorial for forage and moisture.

Bushveld

George J Bredenkamp

Flat-topped thorn trees rooted in fertile, clayey soil and silhouetted against a dusky red sky ...

antelope and zebra roaming warm, rain-drenched, grassy plains. These are the typical images of Africa.

But these same trees are sometimes silhouetted against the fiery red of flames, seething through the dry

grass. And these same antelope flee the devastating fire in haste and confusion. These contrasting

vignettes portray critical elements that act as driving forces in maintaining the integrity of African

savanna, of climate, vegetation, soil fertility, grazing antelopes and fire. This vast area of diverse

habitats, is the epitomy of Africa.

To the north of the Magaliesberg range in the vicinity of Pretoria, and to the west of the Great Escarpment, stretches a vast savanna region that is generally moister than the Kalahari savanna to its west, and situated at higher altitudes and less tropical in character than the lowveld savanna that lies east of the Escarpment. Covering much of the Northern Province and smaller parts of North-West, Gauteng and Mpumalanga, this region is popularly known as the 'bushveld'.

VEGETATION TYPES
Surprisingly few studies on plant communities have been conducted in the central bushveld of South Africa, with most of those that have been done taking place in nature reserves or on game farms, for management planning. Five broad vegetation types have been mapped in the central bushveld recently.

These are sweet bushveld and clay thorn bushveld, which are nutrient-rich, arid savanna types; and mixed bushveld, Waterberg moist mountain bushveld and Soutpansberg arid mountain bushveld, which represent leached, infertile, moist savanna types.

In KwaZulu-Natal two bushveld types occur (if one does not take the Lowveld regions into account), known as the coast-hinterland bushveld and Natal central bushveld, while the Eastern Cape contributes two further bushveld types – the subarid thorn bushveld and the eastern thorn bushveld.

ABOVE FROM LEFT TO RIGHT Bushveld trees growing on nutrient-rich substrates, like this umbrella thorn, are often fine-leaved, but are well armed with spiny thorns to protect themselves from browsing animals; The sicklebush bears exquisite 'chinese lantern' flowers. This small tree encroaches aggressively on ground where the grass cover has been over-grazed and trampled; The dramatic flower heads of Scadoxus puniceus *appear; Trees that grow on nutrient-poor soils, like this silver clusterleaf, are characteristically broad-leaved. They do not carry thorns as they require no special strategies to prevent overutilisation.*

OPPOSITE The strikingly beautiful crimson-breasted shrike, splendid denizen of Acacia *thornveld.*

CONSERVATION

In contrast to the well-conserved Kalahari and lowveld savanna regions of South Africa, which include vast national parks, the central savanna of South Africa, the higher-lying bushveld of KwaZulu-Natal and the bushveld regions of the Eastern Cape are rather poorly conserved, with conservation areas covering less than five per cent of this biome.

The well-known Pilanesberg Nature Reserve, and the lesser-known Madikwe Game Reserve are major conservation areas. Both of these are situated within the North-West Province.

Many smaller conservation areas are scattered throughout the bushveld region, especially in the Waterberg area, such as Marakele National Park, Welgevonden, Lapalala, Touchstone and Mabula, and all of these protect a variety of plant and animal species.

Farming with game for commercial purposes has become a very important economic activity in many bushveld areas. The demand for game for hunting, trophy collection, meat and sport, and general eco-tourism, has placed a monetary value on game.

As a direct result, game farming is arguably the most lucrative land-use option available in many savanna areas. This has resulted in land-owners becoming more conservation-minded.

It is estimated that due to the game farming industry, the bushveld probably supports more head of game today, in the twentieth century, than it did in the whole of the previous century.

The vigorous game farming industry is an excellent illustration of the fact that conservation need not exclude utilisation, and that ultimately conservation is to the benefit of the human species.

Savanna pasturalists often refer to sweet and sour bushveld. This, as is the case in grassland, refers to the nutritional value and acceptability of the predominant grasses to grazing animals. Sweet grass occurring on the fertile savanna soils is preferred and selected by animals, and has a high nutritional value throughout the year. Sour grass, on the other hand, occurs on infertile soils and is often avoided by animals, and loses its nutritional value during winter. The ratio of sweet to sour grasses determines veld condition. Veld with a mixture of sweet and sour grasses is mixed veld, hence the name mixed bushveld.

The geology of the northern South African savannas is quite complex, and plays a significant role in vegetation types. The bushveld basin is composed of a variety of rocks, from archaean granites to volcanic rocks of various ages and origins. Soil types derived from these rocks are therefore equally varied, and this is reflected in an equally diverse vegetation. An interesting example of how soil characteristics may influence the appearance of vegetation, can be noted in the clay thorn bushveld.

A characteristic property of soils in this veld type is a powerful swelling when wet, and equally significant shrinking when dry. This causes cracks in the soil (and also in building structures erected on these soils). This movement in the soil is caused by a physical reaction to water of a particular group of clay minerals, the montmorrilonites, which are found in these soils. The cracking of the soil prunes the roots of the trees. Furthermore, these soils hold moisture very strongly, and water is consequently not readily available to the plants growing there. Together, these two characteristics of the soils give rise to stunted trees – a type of natural bonsai growth.

Grasses, on the other hand, have extensive, finely divided root systems, capable of absorbing adequate water for the relatively small plants. The grasses are less affected by the cracking soil than trees. The fertility of the clayey soils therefore promotes a dense grass layer, which offers excellent sweet grazing.

Sweet bushveld

Sweet bushveld occurs on the fertile soils in the dry and hot valleys of the Limpopo River and its associated tributaries in the northwestern parts of the Northern Province. The thorny, small-leaved vegetation on the fertile soils is often dominated by *Acacia* species, such as blue thorn (*A. erubescens*) and black thorn (*A. mellifera*), as well as sicklebush (*Dichrostachys cinerea*). When the vegetation is overutilised, these thorny species tend to increase at the expense of the grass layer, to form dense, impenetrable thickets. This results in serious management problems for game and cattle farming in the area. Other typical trees include wild raisin (*Grewia flava*), shepherd's tree (*Boscia albitrunca*) and red

bushwillow (*Combretum apiculatum*) – all of which are highly sought after by browsers. Many *Commiphora* species, such as common corkwood (*C. pyracanthoides*), velvet corkwood (*C. mollis*) and zebra-bark corkwood (*C. merkeri*) also occur in this area.

Clay thorn bushveld

This vegetation occurs on flat plains with red or black, fertile, clayey soils, and is dominated by stunted growth forms of *Acacia* species, including umbrella thorn (*A. tortilis*), scented thorn (*A. nilotica*), knob thorn (*A. nigrescens*), red thorn (*A. gerrardii*), ankle thorn (*A. robusta*) and fine thorn (*A. tenuispina*). The fertile soil supports a dense grass layer, offering excellent, sweet grazing, which is palatable throughout the year. The sweet veld is highly sought after by grazing animals, and this can lead to overgrazing and deterioration of the grass layer. This in turn may cause serious bush encroachment.

ABOVE A big spider steals a ride on the head of a leguaan. Leguaans are the largest lizards on the African continent.

ABOVE Young warthogs establish a rank order at an early age by playful sparring. Serious aggression among warthogs is rare.

BEER, JELLY AND LIVING FENCES

*O*ne of the best-known of the bushveld trees is the marula *(Sclerocarya birrea), a handsome, 12-metre tall tree that produces abundant yellow fruit the size of a plum. The fruit is not only nutritious (it contains more vitamin C than an orange) and thirst-quenching, but is used to produce a potent, tasty beer. A good jelly is also produced from the juice and the stone in the fruit contains a delicious nut. The marula is the first indigenous bushveld tree used in a breeding programme to commercially produce cultivars. This is a challenging task, as the trees are unisexual, with separate male and female trees, and seedlings will take many years to produce fruit.*

The Afrikaans vernacular name of the corkwood (Commiphora spp.) trees is 'kanniedood'. This literally means 'cannot die'. It refers to the fact that fence poles made from the stems of these trees easily grow to form 'living fences'. Most species of corkwood produce aromatic resins. Commiphora myrrha from Arabia produces the fragrant myhrr, used as incense. The larvae of the beetle Diamphidia, from which the Bushman (San) people made arrow poison, feed exclusively on corkwood trees.

Mixed bushveld

Mixed bushveld covers the greatest part – 642 600 square kilometres – of the northern savanna area of South Africa. About 60 per cent has been transformed by agriculture and only about three per cent is officially conserved, mostly in smaller nature reserves and private game farms. The vegetation varies from dense, short bushveld to a rather open, tree savanna. On shallow, infertile soils the broad-leaved red bushwillow is the dominant tree, whereas, on deeper, leached sands, the silver clusterleaf (*Terminalia sericea*) becomes dominant.

More fertile, clay-like soils in low-lying situations are usually dominated by small-leaved thorn trees.

Waterberg moist mountain bushveld (sour bushveld)

This is a typical example of moist, infertile savanna, which is well represented on the rugged and rocky Waterberg and Kransberg ranges in the Northern Province. Due to its high proportion of unpalatable grasses, the area has become known as 'sour bushveld'. It is an area of extraordinary scenic beauty, which includes the Marekele National Park as an example of near-pristine mountain bushveld. A great diversity of habitats is created by the rugged mountains, resulting in an equally great variety of plant species. An interesting phenomenon is the presence of many plant species showing affinities with the flora of the Drakensberg, which indicates an ancient link with this range. Examples are common sugarbush (*Protea caffra*) and especially the silver sugarbush (*Protea roupelliae*), and also various grass and herb species such as common russet grass (*Loudetia simplex*), Natal panicum (*Panicum natalensis*), *Vernonia natalensis*, and many others.

ABOVE The agile nagapie or lesser bushbaby emerges from its nest at night.
RIGHT A magnificent kudu bull.

Soutpansberg arid mountain bushveld

This vegetation type occurs on the Soutpansberg mountains in the
Northern Province. It is related to the Waterberg moist mountain
bushveld, but is somewhat drier, and has stronger bushveld, rather
than Drakensberg affinities.

Coast-hinterland bushveld

This veld type – dominated by sweet thorn (*Acacia karroo*) and Nongoni
bristlegrass (*Aristida junciformis*), occurs on hilly terrain in the Melmoth-
Eshowe area, at an altitude of 450 to 900 metres above sea level.

Natal central bushveld

This veld type covers a large part of the KwaZulu-Natal Midlands, at
altitudes ranging from 600 to 1 350 meters above sea level. Common
trees and grasses are paperbark thorn (*Acacia sieberana*), sweet thorn,
scented thorn and common hook-thorn (*Acacia caffra*); common thatch-
grass (*Hyparrhenia hirta*) and hairy tridentgrass (*Tristachya leucothrix*).

Subarid thorn bushveld

Found in relatively low-lying valleys in the Eastern Cape, subarid thorn
bushveld is characterised by sweet thorn trees, red grass (*Themeda
triandra*) and bushveld turpentinegrass (*Cymbopogon plurinodis*).

Eastern thorn bushveld

This veld type occurs along the Eastern Cape coast, extending inland on
dry ridges. The dominant tree is sweet thorn. Eastern thorn bushveld is
invaded by thicket species, and contains some fynbos elements.

ABOVE The majority of succulent plants are small – an adaptation to arid conditions. However, sizeable succulents, such as this naboom, are found in the savannas.

ABOVE RIGHT Early morning sunlight reveals the myriad cracks and crevices on a crag in the Waterberg, a large mountainous complex in the savanna biome.

BELOW The beautiful lilac-breasted roller is an effective hunter of a wide variety of small prey animals, including frogs, lizards and insects.

SURVIVAL STRATEGIES

Some bushveld trees have the ability to produce tannins, causing leaves to become bitter and unpalatable. This strategy is triggered when the leaves of a palatable tree are browsed. At the same, time a chemical message is sent to all the trees in the vicinity, and they all increase tannin production, thus protecting them against overutilisation.

Some trees that belong to the family Euphorbiaceae have highly toxic sap. The production of toxins is also a strategy against overutilisation. For example, the naboom (*Euphorbia ingens*), a large succulent tree, has a white, milky though poisonous latex, while the tamboti (*Spirostachys africana*) is equally notorious as a poisonous tree. Even the dry, dead wood of tamboti contains such a high level of poisonous substances that meat barbecued on a tamboti fire is not suitable for human consumption. However, the black rhinoceros seems unaffected by the tamboti's toxins, and readily browses its leaves. The latex of many *Euphorbia* species was included in arrow poisons of the gatherer-hunters of former times.

A more obvious survival strategy is the development of thorns, and many bushveld plant species have developed stout spines to protect themselves from browsing animals. Thorny species, such as the *Acacias*, are often the dominant plants in fertile, game-rich savannas. Ironically, many of these species depend on browsing animals for the dispersal of their seeds – the fruit and/or seeds are eaten and then deposited via faeces at new sites. Some *Acacia* seeds need to pass through the digestive tracts of animals to stimulate germination.

A number of trees do not need special strategies to prevent over-utilisation. For example, the red bushwillow – while quite palatable, grows in nutrient-poor savanna areas that are not favoured by browsers.

ABOVE A blue wildebeest cow tends her calf.

ABOVE A grey-headed bush shrike forages in a shady tree.

WILDLIFE OF THE SAVANNA BIOME

*O*ver many thousands of years the savanna systems and the antelope that inhabit them have developed side by side. Grasses, for example, have become well adapted to defoliation, as much a defensive response to constant pressure by grazers as to the regular veld fires that raze through the savanna in the dry seasons. The success of grasses has been a constantly renewed vast reservoir of food upon which large herds of grazers flourish. Substantial herds of blue wildebeest (Connochaetus taurinus), Burchell's zebra (Equus burchelli), impala (Aepyceros melampus) and African buffalo (Syncerus caffer), and smaller numbers of antelope such as eland (Taurotragus oryx), red hartebeest (Alcelaphus buselaphus), roan (Hippotragus equinus), sable (H. niger) and tsessebe (Damaliscus lunatus) have therefore become synonomous with savanna.

The savanna is also the habitat of large animals such as elephant (Loxodonta africana) and white rhinoceros (Ceratotherium simum). These, too are an integral component of savanna and many browsers – such as kudu (Tragelaphus strepsiceros), black rhinoceros (Diceros bicornis) and giraffe (Giraffa camelopardalis) – exploit its woody component. And with so many herbivores present, the carnivores also flourish – the big cats such as lion (Panthera leo), leopard (P. pardus) and cheetah (Acinonyx jubatus), as well as many smaller carnivores, are to be seen in the savannas of Africa.

In the more remote parts of the lowveld and Kalahari savannas, large carnivores such as lions and cheetah have survived the depredations of human hunters. Prior to the proclamation of the Kruger National Park, elephant had been hunted almost to extinction in this area, and elephants probably re-established themselves in the South African lowveld from Mozambique. White and black rhinoceros have been saved in the nick of time in the KwaZulu-Natal reserves in the Lowveld, but in the bushveld region of South Africa, these species have been hunted to extinction. Today they have been reintroduced to larger reserves such as Pilanesberg and Madikwe in the North-West Province.

The savanna biome is populated by a greater diversity of bird species than any other biome in South Africa. The presence of both woody plants and a well-developed grass layer provides diverse sources of food and shelter.

Not only are the savanna regions a constant delight for experienced birders, but they are also arguably the ideal first 'hunting-ground' of the budding bird-watcher. The reasons are fairly obvious. More species can be seen than in any other biome, while many bushveld birds are often more colourful and easier to identify than, for instance, many grassland and Karoo birds. Also, the more open terrain means that most bushveld birds are easier to observe than those inhabiting forests and marshes. Some savanna birds are specialists in terms of diet and habitat, whilst others are generalists. For example, the savanna supports many seed-eaters such as doves, sparrows, weavers, waxbills, buntings, canaries and mannikins. The majority of these find their food on the ground, however, some of the smaller seed-eaters may harvest seed whilst clinging to the grass stems.

Fruit-bearing plants account for the presence of barbets, loeries and green pigeons, which find most of their food in the canopies of trees and shrubs.

Insectivores constitute a very large component of the bushveld avifauna, and there is an abundance of francolins, hoopoes, larks, hornbills, shrikes and robins, to name a few major groups that find their prey in every conceivable niche in this rich habitat. Some shrikes, rollers and kingfishers hunt by swooping down from vantage points on trees or bushes to take their prey on the ground, while woodpeckers and wood-hoopoes find their insect prey mainly on or under the bark of tree trunks and thicker branches. Many other savanna species also forage widely among leaves, branches and twigs. These include some of the shrikes, tits, warblers, white-eyes, batises, cuckoos, orioles and bulbuls. Some of the bee-eaters, flycatchers, and nightjars, as well as the drongo, 'hawk' their prey from perches, while swifts, swallows, some nightjars and some raptors hunt 'on the wing'.

Diurnal and nocturnal birds of prey abound, due to the presence of mammalian, avian, reptilian and arthropod prey. If carrion is available, vultures may also be present. Nectar-producing flowers support sunbirds, but are also opportunistically utilised by a wide variety of other birds that normally depend on other food sources. Fish-eaters such as herons, hamerkops, fish eagles and some of the kingfisher species, haunt bushveld rivers and streams. Oxpeckers find ticks on the larger herbivores. And, a unique group, the honeyguides, even eat bees' wax!

Lowveld

Noel van Rooyen

The Lowveld is bound by the low rise of the Lebombo Mountains to the east and the majestic cliffs of the Great Escarpment to the west; and northwards by the Limpopo River valley, and the Tugela River in the south. Scattered trees and shrubs and a continuous ground cover dominated by grass ensures widespread habitation by wildlife, making the Lowveld a prime conservation area. Indeed, approximately 32.3 per cent of the Lowveld area north of Swaziland is under conservation – constituting some 1.85 per cent of the entire southern African region.

VEGETATION TYPES

As outlined previously (see box on pages 14–15), savanna constitutes the largest biome in southern Africa, and as the Lowveld forms part of this biome, many principles mentioned here are applicable to savannas in general. Nine major lowveld vegetation types have been described.

Mopane shrubveld

This occurs on the basalt plains along the Lebombo range in the northern Kruger National Park at altitudes of 300 to 400 metres. The soils are very clayey and the vegetation is dominated by a stunted and multi-stemmed shrubby growth of fairly dense mopane, associated with individuals of leadwood (*Combretum imberbe*) and knob thorn (*Acacia nigrescens*).

Mopane bushveld

Mopane bushveld can be found on undulating landscapes on basalt, granite, sandstone and shale in the northern Kruger National Park at 300 to 700 metres above sea level. In contrast to the mopane shrubveld where the mopane is stunted, this vegetation type is characterised by a fairly dense growth of mopane (*Colophospermum mopane*) trees up to 22 metres in height, mixed with red bushwillow (*Combretum apiculatum*) in many places. Mopane bushveld also occurs in the extreme northern parts of South Africa, north of the Soutpansberg range. The mopane bushveld in South Africa represents the southernmost part of an extensive vegetation type that covers large parts of the hot, low-lying areas of southern tropical Africa.

ABOVE *A spotted hyena pup nibbles on a friend. The spotted hyena is the most common large carnivore in the Kruger National Park.*

BELOW *The graceful nyala.*

Lebombo arid mountain bushveld

As the name suggests, this type of vegetation occurs on the undulating, rocky Lebombo Mountains on the eastern border with Mozambique and in Swaziland, at altitudes ranging from 300 to 400 metres. The most common tree species are Lebombo ironwood (*Androstachys johnsonii*), red bushwillow and knob thorn.

Mixed lowveld bushveld

This bushveld occurs on flat to undulating granitic landscapes between 350 and 500 metres altitude and extends from north to south through the central parts of the Lowveld, forming dense bush on the uplands, open tree savanna in the bottomlands and dense riverine woodland on river banks. Rocky outcrops with large granitic boulders are scattered through this region. The tree layer is characterised by red bushwillow, largefruit bushwillow (*Combretum zeyheri*), knob thorn, sicklebush (*Dichrostachys cinerea*) and silver clusterleaf (*Terminalia sericea*).

Sweet lowveld bushveld

This type of bushveld is found on reasonably flat basaltic plains from 170 to 250 metres above sea level in a narrow strip just west of the Lebombo Mountains. It occurs from the Olifants River in the Kruger Park southwards through Swaziland and into the northern parts of KwaZulu-Natal. This flat, grass-filled, open tree savanna is characterised by marula (*Sclerocarya birrea*), knob thorn, leadwood and sicklebush.

Sour lowveld bushveld

The sour lowveld bushveld is found on the eastern slopes and foothills of the Great Escarpment from the Soutpansberg in the north to Swaziland in the south. It is an undulating, granitic landscape at altitudes of 550 to 800 metres.

This open tree savanna is dominated by silver clusterleaf, bushwillow (*Combretum* spp.) and paperbark thorn (*Acacia sieberana*). High rainfall and a frost-free climate allow a lush vegetation to develop. Around Punda Maria in the northern Kruger National Park a highly diverse and mixed vegetation has developed.

Subhumid lowveld bushveld

This vegetation can be found in the northern parts of KwaZulu-Natal (Ndumo Game Reserve and Tembe Elephant Park), at an altitude of some 100 metres. It is a dense bushveld related to sand forest.

Principal trees are flat-crown (*Albizia adianthifolia*), large-leaf false thorn (*Albizia versicolor*), knob thorn, marula and the giant raisin (*Grewia hexamita*). This bushveld type is shaped by the high rainfall, lack of frost, coupled with deep sandy soils of marine origin, frequent fires and general grazing.

ABOVE *In the mopane veld of the northern Kruger National Park an eland is etched against the rich light of late afternoon. Eland are Africa's largest and heaviest antelopes.*

Coastal bushveld/grassland

Maputaland consists of a mosaic of vegetation types from just above sea level to about 300 metres altitude. The vegetation is conserved in Tembe Elephant Park, Sileza Nature Reserve and Kosi Bay Coastal Forest Reserve. The area is deeply dissected by the many rivers that drain eastwards across KwaZulu-Natal. The remaining forest patches are characterised by species such as forest iron plum (*Drypetes gerrardii*), umzimbeet (*Millettia grandis*) and white ironwood (*Vepris undulata*). Much closer to the seashore, evergreen thicket occurs on littoral dunes. Typical canopy species are coast red milkwood (*Mimusops caffra*), KwaZulu-Natal guarri (*Euclea natalensis*), *Brachylaena discolor* and *Apodytes dimidiata*. The grasslands in this area are unique and often have a shrubby appearance due to many dwarf shrubs such as the dwarf mobola (*Parinari capensis* subsp. *incohata*), *Diospyros galpinii* and *Salacia kraussii*. Locally, at swampy localities, the ilala palm (*Hyphaene coriacea*), is very prominent.

KwaZulu-Natal lowveld bushveld

The KwaZulu-Natal lowveld bushveld covers much of the Lowveld of Zululand that lies between 150 and 450 metres altitude and includes nature reserves such as Hluhluwe, Umfolozi and Mkuzi. The vegetation is a mixture of thicket and open bushveld. The most common tree species include umbrella thorn (*Acacia tortilis*), sweet thorn (*Acacia karroo*) and red bushwillow. Where disturbance is less severe, grass species such as red grass (*Themeda triandra*) dominate.

CLIMATE AND GEOLOGY

The climate of the Lowveld is essentially subtropical, with wet summers and dry winters. The northern areas have an annual precipitation of 375 to 600 millimetres, increasing to 750 millimetres in the southwest. November is often the hottest month, when temperatures above 40°C are not uncommon. The winters are generally mild and stretch from May to the end of August.

ABOVE On a misty May morning, an inquisitive giraffe stands motionless in a game path. A red-billed oxpecker clings to its cheek, searching for ticks.

The geology of the northern Lowveld is relatively uncomplicated. The western part is mostly of granitic origin, and going eastwards changes to thin sections of shale and sandstone, then basalt on the flat plains, to the rhyolitic Lebombo Mountains to the east. East of the Lebombo Mountains cretaceous sediments consisting of grey and red sands can be found. In certain parts, dolerite and gabbro intrusions are found while sandstone occurs in the extreme north.

KRUGER NATIONAL PARK

Covering almost 20 000 square kilometres, the Kruger Park is one of the largest national parks in the world. It represents about 20 per cent of all conserved land in South Africa. The park stretches a full 350 kilometres from north to south, and 90 kilometres from west to east at its widest point. The fences between the Kruger National Park and the private reserves to the west of it have recently been taken down, resulting

the greatest attraction is the atmosphere of wilderness and isolation. In the far north, multi-coloured sandstone hills occur amongst magnificent baobabs (*Adansonia digitata*), while it is one of the few places in South Africa where tropical riverine forests and dense groves of fever trees can be found.

Biodiversity

The Kruger National Park has an impressive biological diversity and a natural richness that few of the world's other great national parks can match. Nearly 150 mammal species have been recorded, including six of the seven cat species found in Africa. The bird life is prolific, with more than 500 species having been documented. Other creatures, too, are well represented. Thus 119 reptile species, 51 fish species and 35 amphibians are known to occur in the park, while spiders, scorpions and insects abound.

Plantlife

Plantlife is rich and varied, from tropical to subtropical, with more than 2 000 plant species having been identified, including some 450 tree and shrub species, and 235 grasses. The number of tree species is almost half the number of the total tree flora of South Africa. A large number of vegetation types (plant communities) have been described and mapped for the Kruger National Park, and related types have been synthesised into 35 landscapes which are used as management units.

From an ecotourism point of view, the Kruger National Park is delineated into 16 natural areas (or ecozones), each of these being relatively homogeneous regarding their geology, land form, rainfall, vegetation and animals. The vegetation of the southern half, and a small area in the extreme north of the Kruger National Park is very varied.

However, the most prominent feature of much of the northern half of the park is the almost monotonous dominance of mopane shrubs and trees. The leaves and pods of these trees provide important fodder to many animals. The mopane bushveld is often regarded as synonymous with elephant *(Loxodonta africana)*, as this vegetation type is favoured by these animals. Also associated with the mopane is a colourful, spiny caterpillar of a large moth *Gonimbrasia belina*, which feeds exclusively on mopane leaves. These caterpillars – 'mopane worms' – are a source of protein and are eagerly sought after by African people. Dried and roasted, and even canned in peri-peri sauce, the mopane worms form an important component of their diet.

The giant of savanna trees, the boabab, is easily recognised by its extreme girth and dominating appearance. They dot the mopane landscape and rugged hills of the Pafuri area, but scattered individuals occur as far south as Tshokwane. Although baobabs are only up to about 15 metres tall, their trunk circumference can vary from eight to 30 metres. Their flowers

in a larger, continuous conservation area. World famous for its diverse and abundant wildlife, the park is more than just a place to see lions, elephants and a spectrum of other animals. Its magnificent scenery and unique wildness make it one of the few remaining areas of South Africa where unspoilt Africa can be experienced.

Although mainly flat, with vast grassy plains, it also has undulating and mountainous regions covered by a diversity of plant species. Perhaps

ABOVE A lion cub plays with a stick. This will help to hone his hunting skills.

are pollinated by bats. Baobab fruit is sought after by animals and local people. Legend has it that there is no such a thing as a young baobab. This is probably due to the fact that the young trees, and especially their leaves, are so different in appearance from the mature trees that they are not recognised as the same species. Baobabs have extraordinary soft wood, and are therefore very vulnerable to destruction by elephants. Old dying trees will eventually topple, soon disintegrating into a mound of fibrous pulp. An individual Boabab tree is indeed a small ecosystem on its own, with many insects, birds and other animals living in its branches, feeding on its leaves, flowers, fruit and even its stem and bark.

Wildlife

With nearly 150 species recorded, the Kruger National Park is an unbelievable treasure house of mammal species. Of the larger mammals, the species occurring in the greatest numbers are impala (*Aepyceros*

ABOVE A triumphant male lion rests for a few minutes next to a giraffe carcass.

melampus) – more than 150 000, Burchell's zebra (*Equus burchelli*) – more than 30 000, African buffalo (*Syncerus caffer*) – more than 20 000, blue wildebeest (*Connochaetus taurinus*) – nearly 14 000, and elephant – more than 9 000.

Species such as giraffe (*Giraffa camelopardalis*), kudu (*Tragelaphus strepsiceros*), waterbuck (*Kobus ellipsiprymus*), warthog (*Phacochoerus aethiopicus*), hippopotamus (*Hippopotamus amphibius*), bushbuck (*Tragelaphus scriptus*), reedbuck (*Redunca arundinum*), and white rhinoceros (*Ceratotherium simum*) occur in lower numbers.

The white rhinoceros – which was locally extinct and was reintroduced – is doing very well, with its numbers exceeding 1 800 animals. Nyala (*Tragelaphus angasi*), sable (*Hippotragus niger*), eland (*Taurotragus oryx*) and tsessebe (*Damaliscus lunatus*) occur in numbers of less than 1 000 individuals per species.

The black rhinoceros (*Diceros bicornis*) population is estimated at 300 animals. Of the larger predators, the spotted hyena (*Crocuta crocuta*) is the most common (at around 2 000), followed by lion (*Panthera leo*) (approximately 1 500). The stealthy leopard (*P. pardus*) is difficult to census, and the Kruger Park population is estimated to number somewhere between 600 and 900 individuals.

The numbers of cheetah (*Acinonyx jubatus*) and wild dog (*Lycaon pictus*) are very low, in the vicinity of 250 to 350 individuals per species.

Elephants are the largest terrestrial animals living today. The elephant is synonymous with untamed Africa, and a flagship species in the conservation struggle. However, their numbers in Africa are under grave threat since they dropped from at least three million a century ago to less than 600 000 in 1991. This decline was brought about by growing human numbers and the ivory trade.

However, since the ban in the international ivory trade in 1989 the incidence of ivory poaching has declined, and in conservation areas of the southern African states, elephant numbers are increasing. The Kruger National Park is home to probably the largest ivory carriers

ABOVE The strikingly handsome sable bull sports a magnificent set of horns and a glossy black coat.

in Africa. So impressive was the ivory of certain old bulls – Shingwedzi, Shawu, Dzombo, Ndlulamithi, Kambaku, Mafunyane and Joao – that in their time they became famous as the 'Magnificent Seven'.

Elephant numbers in the Lowveld were reduced by hunters during the previous century. Around 1912 a herd of about 25 elephants was known to have settled along the Shingwedzi River. Since then their numbers have increased to approximately 7 000 in the late 1960s. The management policy until recently was to maintain the Kruger National Park elephant population at around 7 000 to 7 500, with annual culling of excess animals. since culling has been discontinued the elephant numbers have increased to more than 9 000. Adult elephants consume between 150 and 300 kilograms of plant material over 24 hours and an average of about 200 litres of water in the same period.

Although some plant species (such as the baobab) display evidence of heavy utilisation, no habitat in the Kruger Park has shown signs of excessive elephant damage and no species, either plant or animal, is known to have disappeared due to the presence and activity of too many elephants. Other methods of ensuring the elephant's survival are being researched, as well as alternatives to culling. Translocation of entire

CONSERVATION THREATS IN THE LOWVELD

The Lowveld faces two main threats: a diminishing water supply and a rapidly expanding, impoverished human population. Few of the major rivers that flow through the Lowveld rise in the Lowveld itself. The vast commercial plantations of exotic pines and eucalypts on the Escarpment may appear innocuous to the passerby, but these plantations destroy the vital montane grasslands, which are not only rich in diversity of endemic plant and animal life, but act as a natural filter and feeder of water into the Lowveld's major rivers. The waters that reach the plains are further drawn for irrigation of farmlands, industry and domestic use.

Water is becoming an increasingly scarce strategic resource, demanding optimal management.

The Lowveld, and particularly the Kruger National Park, is located downstream of the relevant rivers, which makes it vulnerable to the quantity and quality of water and sediment loads. The goals of the Kruger Park's River Research Programme, initiated in 1987, are to predict the impact of changing flow regimes and water quality as basis for managing water for ecological purposes.

Major rivers such as the Limpopo, Levuvhu, Letaba, Olifants, Sabie, Crocodile, Komati and Pongola were perennial before man intervened.

In recent years some of them have been reduced to a trickle or have ceased flowing altogether. If any river is altered in such a way that it ceases to exist as a dynamic ecosystem, then an essential component of the Lowveld as an ecosystem will be lost.

There is a need for the sustainable use of our natural environment, especially with a burgeoning and largely impoverished population on the borders of the Lowveld's game reserves. Outside the conservation areas the population is in need of firewood, building and fencing materials. Thatching grass, reeds, wild fruits, medicinal plants and other natural products contribute to the economy of the area and the well-being of people. The sprawling rural communities on the borders of conservation areas and other parks were mostly precluded from involvement with management and economic or social benefits. Questions of whether cattle and other farming would not be more relevant activities have been raised. Sub-subsistence farmers ask whether the preservation and protection of animals and natural vegetation are of more importance than human beings? It would, however, prove nothing to open those protected places to human settlement on a large scale as overutilisation would soon become evident. An alternative is ecotourism, a sustainable industry that has tremendous potential for generating revenue and employment. The local communities benefit materially from tourist resources – an approach successfully used in KwaZulu-Natal. The management of the Kruger Park is currently committed to identifying with the needs of those on its borders and to drawing them into general interdependence and prosperity for the region.

Pollution and waste disposal are also growing problems, particularly in large urban centres and need to be addressed before they despoil vital resources such as clean air and water.

ABOVE A young leopard stares momentarily into the lens. Once they have reached maturity, leopards lead solitary lives. Males and females only come together to mate.

family groups, instead of groups of juveniles, as well as population control by contraception are encouraged as alternatives.

Lions still remain the greatest attraction in the Kruger Park, which supports some of the highest numbers and densities of lions anywhere in Africa. Some of the largest prides have also been reported from the Kruger Park – one pride studied near Satara camp consisted of 39 individuals. Because of the denser nature of the vegetation, however, the Kruger Park lions may be more difficult to locate than those in more open areas like the Kalahari and some of the East African reserves. Compared to the Kalahari lions, lowveld lions consistently kill larger prey, such as wildebeest, zebra and impala species. Having said this, researchers have, by dividing kill frequency by the relative abundance of the various prey species, suggested that the waterbuck is the preferred prey species of the Kruger Park lions.

On the other hand, if one considers the biomass of animals killed, the giraffe is the most important prey species, followed by wildebeest, zebra,

buffalo, impala, kudu, and waterbuck. Giraffe meat accounts for nearly 30 per cent of a lion's food consumption. Overall, however, the lion is an opportunist and will kill what is available. At least 37 mammal species, some birds (even ostriches – *Struthio camelus*), and reptiles including small crocodiles *(Crocodylus niloticus)*, have been recorded as lion prey.

With more than 500 recorded species, the Kruger National Park is one of the most productive areas for birdwatching in South Africa. Because tropical savanna is so widespread in Africa, however, the Kruger Park is not the place to look for South African endemics.

The park is, however, of great interest to ornithologists on three counts. Firstly, the sheer diversity of species is rivalled only by the richest bird-watching areas in the far northern KwaZulu-Natal lowveld and the Nylsvlei area in the bushveld. Second, a number of species that were previously far more widespread in South Africa, are now most easily observed in the Kruger Park. Outside reserves, these birds are often subjected to direct persecution by farmers because they are predators

ABOVE A herd of Cape buffalo thunders off in a dry river course. Disease and climatological factors affecting habitat, rather than predation by lions, regulate the numbers of buffalo populations.

BELOW Inquisitive buffalo investigate the photographer's vehicle.

and are perceived as threats to livestock. Also, they are used in traditional medicinal or occult practices, while some species are taken for food. They may also be indirectly persecuted, for instance by exposure to poisons used to control other animals. Large eagles and vultures immediately spring to mind as examples of formerly more widespread species.

Both the spectacular martial eagle (*Polemaetus bellicosus*) and bateleur (*Terathopius ecaudatus*) still occur in healthy populations in the Kruger National Park and adjacent conservation areas, while their numbers have dramatically declined elsewhere. (Significant populations of these two species also occur in the Kalahari Gemsbok National Park and the northern KwaZulu-Natal reserves.) Other large birds like the kori bustard (*Ardeotis kori*) and ground hornbill (*Bucorvus leadbeateri*) are also for the most part confined to bigger conservation areas today.

The same is true of the two oxpecker species (*Buphagus* spp.). Since their food source consists almost exclusively of ticks, they cannot survive in farming areas where cattle are regularly dipped in highly toxic fluids.

ABOVE LEFT, RIGHT Wild dogs feed on an impala; Beyond the reach of lions and hyenas in the safety of an apple-leaf tree, a leopard feasts on its grey duiker kill.

BELOW The silvery beard of a Burchell's zebra is highlighted by the early morning sun.

The third reason why the Lowveld – and the Kruger Park in particular – is of special ornithological importance, is the fact that many tropical African birds reach their southernmost distribution here. Because birds are so mobile, some stragglers and vagrants occasionally turn up in strange places. But, in general, the Lowveld is the South African mainstay of such striking tropical species as the saddle-billed stork (*Ephippiorhynchus senegalensis*), open-billed stork (*Anastomus lamelligerus*), marabou stork (*Leptoptilos crumeniferus*), Dickinson's kestrel (*Falco dickinsoni*), Pel's fishing owl (*Scotopelia peli*), white-crowned plover (*Vanellus albiceps*), Böhm's spinetail (*Neafrapus boehmi*), mottled spinetail (*Telacanthura ussheri*), broad-billed roller (*Eurystomus glaucurus*), mosque swallow (*Hirundo senegalensis*), wattle-eyed flycatcher (*Platysteira peltata*), yellow-spotted nicator (*Nicator gularis*), tropical boubou (*Laniarius aethiopicus*), and long-tailed starling (*Lamprotornis mevesii*). Some of these species have restricted ranges in the Kruger National Park, and the Pafuri region in the far north is famous among birders as the most reliable spot to locate many of them.

Private Game Reserves

Since the 1970s, a cattle-free and carefully managed group of privately owned game reserves have developed along the western border of the Kruger National Park. In recent years, the fence separating the private reserves from the park has been removed, providing greater freedom of movement for the game and restoring migration routes. The entire area is under joint management.

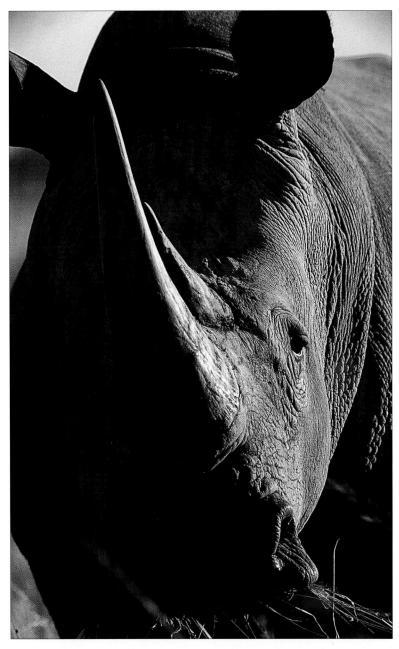

BELOW A white rhino in close-up. Hunted to the brink of extinction elsewhere in Africa, South Africa still has healthy populations of both white and black rhinoceros. The KwaZulu-Natal parks played a key role in rhino conservation.

The privately owned game reserves are mainly used for game-viewing. Managers of these reserves operate in an ecologically sensitive area and believe the only way to provide facilities for tourists without degrading the land is to have a low-density, though high-tariff operation.

KWAZULU-NATAL LOWVELD

Some of the oldest conservation areas in southern Africa can be found in the lowveld savanna region of KwaZulu-Natal.

LOWVELD DISEASES

Anthrax

One of the scourges of the Kruger Park is anthrax, a bacterial disease endemic in the northern areas of the park. Occasional epidemics occur, especially during very dry seasons. Unfortunately some of the rare animal species such as roan antelope (Hippotragus equinus), are very susceptible to the disease. An immunisation programme was started in the 1970s to ensure survival of these animals. Their numbers are nevertheless slowly decreasing due to disease, drought, predation and competition from other grazers. Tsessebe (Damaliscus lunatis) are also rare and susceptible to disease and predation.

Foot-and-mouth

Foot-and-mouth is endemic to the Lowveld, and buffalo (Syncerus caffer) are the major carriers of the disease. During the early 1960s veterinary cordon fences were erected on the western border of the Kruger Park to contain outbreaks of foot-and-mouth in cattle farming areas. The fence had an unfortunate side-effect. It cut across ancient migration routes, and led to a population crash of some wildlife species, in particular, blue wildebeest (Connochaetus taurinus). Fortunately the wildebeest population stabilised, although at much lower numbers, and they established new migration patterns.

Ironically the fence was later lifted when private nature reserves west of Kruger were incorporated into the park. A fence was erected in 1976 along the eastern border between the Kruger National Park and Mozambique, but it interfered mainly with elephant movements. The elephants were more adaptable and did not suffer any population reductions. Today, foot-and-mouth is still a problem in Kruger, and as a result there are strict limitations on the export of live animals and animal products from this park.

Malaria

Malaria, a serious parasitic disease carried by infected female Anopheles mosquitos, is endemic to the Lowveld. Some strains of malaria can be fatal, and if uncontrolled, the spread of malaria could lead to economic decline and a decreased tourist potential.

Sleeping sickness and nagana

The tsetse fly is a carrier of a deadly parasite (Trypanosome), which causes sleeping sickness in man and nagana in cattle. Because of this threat to people and the desire to improve land use for a burgeoning population, tsetse fly control dates back to the 1940s. Control methods used were rather extreme and destructive, and included the large-scale slaughtering of game, and habitat destruction (ring-barking and bush clearing). Later, insecticides such as DDT, Dieldrin and Endosulphan, were used. Fortunately, sleeping sickness and nagana do not pose a threat in South Africa today.

ABOVE A group of hippopotamuses lounge in the shallow water of the Sabie River, while red-billed oxpeckers search their hides for ectoparasites.

BELOW In an orange haze of the late afternoon sun, blue wildebeest graze the sweet grass of the central plains of the Kruger National Park.

Once the hunting preserve of Zulu kings, the Hluhluwe section of the Hluhluwe-Umfolozi Park is now a conservation area that offers visitors unforgettable viewing of many animals and birds. This reserve is one of the oldest in Africa and was established in 1895 along with the Umfolozi and St Lucia reserves.

The reserve is named after the thorny monkey rope (*Dalbergia armata*), used by the Zulus to muzzle their calves during weaning. Nestled among foothills rising from the coastal plain the hills and plains offer an unusual combination of forest, woodland, savanna and grassland found only rarely in Africa.

The semideciduous forests are also specific and distinctive features of the KwaZulu-Natal lowveld area. In the Mbhombe Forest trees such as the strangler fig (*Ficus thonningii*), the Natal milk plum (*Englerophytum natalense*), the scented thorn (*Acacia nilotica*), and the Camdeboo stinkwood (*Celtis africana*) are found.

ABOVE FROM LEFT TO RIGHT *The charming, fat little barred owl is not strictly nocturnal; A delicately-hued green pigeon clambers around in a wild fig tree, feasting on the ripening fruits; The Kruger Park and the KwaZulu-Natal reserves are important havens for large birds of prey. Here an adult martial eagle rests in a shady tree.*
BELOW *An armoured ground cricket making its way through the summer grasses.*

While St Lucia to the east is a separate geographic entity, the Hluhluwe and Umfolozi reserves have been joined together when the broad corridor that once separated them was included in a combined reserve comprising almost 1 000 square kilometres.

Although less than six per cent of the size of the Kruger National Park, it boasts about two-thirds of the total number of plant species found in Kruger. The so-called 'big five' – elephant, lion, leopard, buffalo, and rhinoceros (both black and white) – all occur here.

The Umfolozi section of the reserve was named after the White and Black Mfolozi rivers that meander through the area before reaching a confluence on the eastern border. About half of this section of the reserve is a wilderness area accessible only on foot. The Umfolozi reserve is sometimes remembered for a sad episode in its history – the slaughter of more than 70 000 head of game during the 1940s in a futile attempt to control the tsetse fly. The fly was eventually eradicated by aerial spraying.

Today the reserve is best known for the successful fight to save the white rhino. The area teems with wildlife and no fewer than 48 species of large mammals, 37 species of reptiles, nine species of amphibians, more than 400 species of birds and 136 different butterflies are found.

In 1985, elephant were reintroduced to Hluhluwe-Umfolozi Park, from the Kruger National Park.

The extreme northern part of KwaZulu-Natal is known as Maputaland. It is a low-lying sandy plain that once formed part of the sea bed, but is today covered in a mosaic of savanna, sand forest, marshes, floodplains, pans and lakes.

Scattered through Maputaland are several fascinating conservation areas boasting an exceptionally high biodiversity. Mkuzi and Ndumo game reserves are both especially famous for their profusion of bird life.

In 1983 the Tembe Elephant Park was specially proclaimed to protect the last free-ranging elephants in KwaZulu-Natal.

ABOVE LEFT The yellow-billed hornbill is one of the most comical, and most characteristic, denizens of the savanna areas.

ABOVE RIGHT Drinking at a rainwater puddle among fallen mopane leaves, the plumage of two greater blue-eared glossy starlings sparkles with irridescent splendour.

BELOW Much of the northern parts of the Lowveld are covered in mopane scrub or trees – here a breathtaking sight in their dry-season colours.

ABOVE *The Kruger National Park has, in its time, been sanctuary to some of the largest ivory-bearing elephants in Africa.*

Centred on the largest estuary in South Africa, the Greater St Lucia Wetland Park is richly endowed with terrestrial as well as aquatic life forms. Kosi Bay and Lake Sibaya are other unspoilt wetlands of the region. The Phinda Resource Reserve is the result of a modern initiative combining up-market ecotourism with sustainable utilisation of natural resources to the benefit of local people.

Bird life

Many consider the northern reserves of KwaZulu-Natal to be the most rewarding area for bird-watching in South Africa. Ndumo, Mkuzi and parts of the St Lucia complex are particularly highly rated.

Exciting 'specials' of the area include southern banded snake eagle (*Circaetus fasciolatus*), the fruit-eating palm-nut vulture (*Gypohierax angolensis*), the Natal nightjar (*Caprimulgus natalensis*), Rudd's apalis (*Apalis ruddi*), Woodward's batis (*Batis fratrum*), the exquisite

Neergaard's sunbird (*Nectarinia neergaardi*) and the pretty pink-throated twinspot (*Hypargos margaritatus*).

BIODIVERSITY AND ENDEMISM IN THE LOWVELD

Although lowveld savanna is not renowned for its endemism, there are pockets that have been identified by scientists as 'centres of endemism', for example, the Maputaland Centre of Endemism along the east of the Lebombo Mountains, and the Barberton Centre.

More than 2 500 species of vascular plants occur in the Maputaland Centre, and of these at least 225 species or infraspecific taxa and three genera are endemic/near-endemic to the region.

The area is exceptional for its animal diversity, which includes many endemics spread over the whole biotic spectrum. On the borders of the Lowveld other centres of endemism are found such as the Soutpansberg and Wolkberg Centres of Endemism.

ABOVE Athlete of the animal world, a cheetah speeds with graceful bounds through the tall winter grass. Fastest of the land mammals, the cheetah is built for speed, not strength.

CONSERVATION MANAGEMENT IN THE KRUGER NATIONAL PARK

Research in the Kruger National Park is aimed at the interrelated cycles of life in the park, from dragonflies to elephants. The knowledge gained helps with the management of soil, vegetation and animal life in the park; it provides information for other conservation areas with fewer scientific resources; it provides vital information for nearby nature reserves and game farms; and it provides fascinating information about natural history that adds significantly to the visitor's enjoyment.

The numbers of different animals in the Kruger National Park change from year to year for many reasons, among which rainfall and the availability of food are the most important. Each year Kruger National Park scientists do a count of the larger herbivores, which is then used in management decision-making. Animal numbers in the park are not entirely self-adjusting and have to be managed. The plant material can only support a given

animal biomass and wise management of the vegetation is essential to maximise its carrying capacity. Savanna can not be regarded as a self-adjusting system, and increased demographic and economic pressure, lead to land degradation. The need for man sometimes to intervene in order to help maintain the sustainable ratio is one which raises all sorts of moral and ethical questions. The need for culling still remains a controversial subject among conservationists and wildlife enthusiasts. The root of the problem is simply that, in spite of its size, the park is essentially a fenced area that needs to be controlled and managed.

The prospect of a possible transfrontier park with Mozambique is currently under investigation. Such a park will contribute substantially to tourism, and animal migration opportunities will relieve grazing pressure on the Kruger National Park.

Rivers and Wetlands

Jay L Walmsley and R Danny Walmsley

By and large, South Africa is a dry country with an irregular and unpredictable rainfall. Water

is arguably the country's most precious natural resource. The flow of even the biggest rivers can slow

dramatically in dry times, and many are reduced to sandy ribbons twisting through the landscape when

rain is scarce. Extensive wetland systems too are few and far between and many of them, like the

rivers and their estuaries, face severe threats from degradation. The conservation of water

resources is of the highest priority.

Water is the most abundant resource on earth, covering 71 per cent of the planet's surface. Its total volume is immense, about 1.4 billion cubic kilometres – and if this volume were spread evenly over the earth's surface, it would form a layer almost three kilometres in depth. Unfortunately, it is estimated that about 97 per cent of this volume is contained in the world's oceans and inland seas, most of which is too salty for drinking and the growing of crops.

Only three per cent is fresh water, and of this three per cent, nearly 90 per cent is contained in ice caps, glaciers, soil and the atmosphere.

These facts tell us the disheartening news that there is a great deal of water on earth, but relatively little present in rivers, wetlands and lakes. In fact, less than one per cent is available to man. To compound the problem the primary source of fresh water is rainfall, of which more than 65 per cent evaporates. Fortunately the hydrological cycle ensures that there is a continual replenishment of water to land surfaces.

WATER, THE ESSENCE OF LIFE

Since the beginning of civilisation, man has been influenced by the need and availability of water. Much of the daily life of early civilisations was centered around oases, springs, rivers, wetlands and lakes. Rivers in particular played a key role in sociocultural life, not only by providing water for crop irrigation, transport systems and domestic needs, but also by contributing to the essence of religious activities. Examples of this are

ABOVE A young hippopotamus in Ensumo Pan in the Mkuzi Game Reserve. Baby hippos weigh about 300 kilograms at birth, and are able to swim within minutes of being born.

RIGHT A saddle-billed stork pauses in a seasonal stream filled with water lilies, in the Kruger National Park.

the Nile in Egypt and the Ganges in India, both of which have, from time immemorial, contributed to the ways of life in these countries. Likewise, the colonisation of America, Africa and Australia by early European settlers, was influenced by the distribution of major aquatic systems, which provided drinking water, food and transportation.

On a global scale, water vapour acts as a protective blanket not only by screening the earth from dangerous ultraviolet radiation from the sun, but also by contributing to maintaining the heat balance of our planet.

By contrast, on a molecular level, water provides a medium within which most of life's physiological and biochemical processes take place.

All living organisms thus depend on water for their basic health and survival. However, the earth's living species do not all require the same amounts of water. For example, fish and many amphibians are entirely dependent on the continual presence of large quantities of water, whereas desert rodents, insects and plants can survive for lengthy periods of time in a dry environment.

AQUATIC ECOREGIONS
On the basis of natural conditions and the characteristics of rivers and wetlands, five southern African ecoregions may be defined.

Subtropical coastal plain
The subtropical coastal plain incorporates the Mpumalanga lowveld, Mozambique and northern KwaZulu-Natal. The marine influence is strong, and aquatic ecosystems have variable salinity.

Summer rainfall regions

The summer rainfall region of the Highveld and southeastern coastal plain, incorporating Gauteng, the North-West Province, the Free State, southern KwaZulu-Natal and the northern section of the Eastern Cape. The Vaal-Orange, Tugela and Limpopo rivers are all included within this region.

Alpine mountain region

The alpine mountain region of Lesotho, in which many major South African rivers have their origins. This area experiences high rainfall, and is characterised by clear mountain streams.

Western and southern Cape mediterranean climate region

This area is one of winter rainfall, with temperate, unbuffered (that is, dilute and sensitive to change in pH) acid waters arising principally from the Table Mountain sandstone in the mountainous regions. Marine influences in the low-lying areas increase the buffering capacity (resistance to change in pH) of waters and raise the pH level. There are two types of waters: the 'peat-stained', acid waters draining the seaward slopes (for instance the Steenbras, Palmiet and Storms rivers), and the colourless acid waters draining from the land-facing slopes (such as the Olifants, Great Berg and Breede rivers).

The arid western region

The arid western region stretches north from inland of Port Elizabeth into Namibia and southern Botswana. The western part of this region is dry. Waters are temporary, alkaline and carry very high dissolved solids and sediment loads. The eastern section is characterised by short, steep, geologically young rivers with permanent flows, neutral to alkaline waters, and moderate levels of dissolved solids.

INFLUENCES ON THE AQUATIC ENVIRONMENT

The characteristics of any country's aquatic ecosystems are largely determined by the interaction between climate, rainfall and the landscape over which water flows.

There are many factors that determine the quality and amount of water entering the hydrological cycle over any particular region. These include continental features, marine influences, latitude, altitude, geology, topography, and so forth. For South Africa, the warm Agulhas Current on the east coast, the cold Benguela Current on the west coast, coupled with the topography of the subcontinent, have created an overall theme of aridity.

South Africa's aquatic ecosystems are subjected to extremely harsh natural conditions, and a number of features naturally affect the country's aquatic environment. These include low precipitation – with an average

ABOVE A dragonfly rests on a broken reed in a Highveld marsh. Dragonflies are some of the oldest flying creatures known – fossil dragonflies have been found dating back 300 million years – preceding the pterodactyl by 100 million years, and the earliest birds by 150 million years.

rainfall of 497 millimetres, the country is well below the world average of 860 millimetres – and high solar radiation due to a low degree of cloudiness. High temporal climatic variability with distinct seasonal rainfall patterns, high spatial climatic variability (the country has six rainfall regions), and generally high evaporation rates are also influential natural conditions. Because a considerable percentage of rainfall is absorbed into the soil, there is a low run-off into rivers.

This is exacerbated by a high variability in river flow (few river systems flow all year round). Severe and prolonged droughts are often terminated by severe floods; at the same time, during any one season, one area of the country may be experiencing drought while another area may be simultaneously subjected to severe flooding.

Another factor influencing South Africa's water resources is the country's development. South Africa is one of the most industrialised countries in Africa, producing almost 50 per cent of the continent's electricity and its population of some 40.5 million is expanding at

an annual rate of about 2.4 per cent. Development has had an enormous impact on the way that surface water is managed.

The major goal of water resource developers over the last 40 years has been to harness utilisable surface water resources and to make this water available to major economic sectors and socio-economic regions of South Africa. One of the main objectives has been the provision of water to mining and industrial activities within the Gauteng area, which contributes over 38 per cent of the country's Gross National Product and contains 18 per cent of the population. Development of the area has proceeded despite the fact that the Vaal River catchment from which it receives its water, only generates eight per cent of the country's surface water run-off. To achieve these objectives, there exists a countrywide net-work of impoundments (dams) that together contain more than 50 per cent of the available surface water run-off. Interbasin transfer schemes trans-port water from catchments of surplus, like the Tugela and Orange rivers, to those of deficit, such as the Vaal and the Fish rivers respectively.

ABOVE The Pafuri region lies in the hottest and driest section of the Kruger National Park. Here the Levhuvhu River supports magnificent riparian vegetation. Increasing degradation of the rivers flowing through the Kruger has become the greatest conservation headache in South Africa's flagship national park.

RIVERS AND RIVER ZONES

There are 22 primary drainage regions in South Africa, each containing a network of river systems of varying length and water flow. All these rivers exhibit physical changes as they flow across the landscape from mountain areas to the sea. Mountain catchment streams are typically narrow, fast-flowing and stony, with well-oxygenated, cool and relatively clear water. By contrast, in reaches of the same river as it nears the coast the flow is slow, the channel is wider and the water much more turbid, warm and less oxygenated.

In South Africa, five typical zones have been identified in the different river systems, but very seldom are they all found in one river. These zones are known as mountain source and cliff waterfalls, mountain streams, foothill sandbeds, low and midland streams and rivers, and estuaries. There are considerable differences in organisms and biodiversity of these different zones. For instance, organisms found in mountain streams do not have as high a pollution tolerance as those of

lower reaches. A good example of this is the exotic trout, which can only survive in the clear, cold, well-oxygenated mountain streams of the Great Escarpment and Western Cape, as opposed to barbel and carp, which thrive in lower reaches.

WETLANDS

A wetland is defined by the Ramsar Convention (Convention on Wetlands of International Importance Especially as Water Fowl Habitat, 1971) as an area of marsh, fen, peatland or water, natural or artificial, permanent or temporary, with water that is static or flowing, fresh, brackish or salt, the depth of which does not exceed six metres. This definition embraces systems such as coastal lakes, estuaries, endorheic (inwardly draining) pans, vleis, flood plains and even certain reservoirs.

Throughout the world, wetlands have been recognised as key habitats for ecological, hydrological and economic reasons. Economic benefits include fisheries, agricultural production, and recreation. They are also

ABOVE Mangrove trees colonise saline coastal swampland, where little else will grow. This ability to grow in sea water – their roots are fully immersed at high tide – is their most extraordinary characteristic.

invaluable in erosion and pollution control, flood attenuation, water storage, stream flow regulation, nutrient assimilation and sediment accretion. Wetlands in the arid South Africa landscape, can be compared to oases in the desert. They provide extremely productive habitats in which moist soils stimulate the growth of plants which, in turn, provide conditions conducive to the establishment of biologically diverse populations of animals and microorganisms.

Four different wetland categories exist in South Africa:

River source sponges
These are found at high altitudes in mountain areas (such as in the Lesotho Highlands).

Marshes and swamps
Marshes and swamps can be further subdivided into sedge marshes, restio marshes, reedbed marshes, reed swamps, papyrus swamps, Cape wetlands, swamp forests, salt marshes and mangrove swamps.

Flood plains
The well-known flood plains of South Africa include the Pongola and Nylsvlei flood plains.

Endorheic pans
These inwardly draining pans with no outlet to the sea comprise salt pans, temporary pans, grass pans, sedge pans, reed pans, and semi-permanent lakes (such as Soutpan and Barbers Pan).

THREATENED AQUATIC ECOSYSTEMS
South Africa has a natural heritage of which aquatic ecosystems form an invaluable part. However, there are many wetalnd systems that are under threat from encroaching development and poor management.

Langebaan Lagoon
Langebaan Lagoon, about 100 kilometres north of Cape Town on the west coast, is a highly unusual wetland ecosystem. It is more like a landlocked arm of the sea than an estuary. Although it has only marine organisms living in it, it functions as an estuary because of its wide mud flats and extensive salt marshes. It is also not quite as saline as the sea due to freshwater seepage.

Truly a remarkable ecosystem, Langebaan Lagoon supports more than 550 invertebrate species in the estuary and Saldanha Bay – almost double the number of invertebrate species recorded for any other estuary in South Africa. In the summer, an astonishing 55 000 waterbirds frequent the lagoon. Although the Langebaan Lagoon and some of its surrounding areas have been set aside as a national park, it is threatened by port and

ABOVE *The mightiest river must be born as a small stream or a number of small streams, or a spongy, highlying marsh.*

BOTTOM RIGHT *Lake St Lucia is the largest estuary in South Africa. It is a unique wetland endowed with a spectacular diversity of plant and animal life.*

industrial development in Saldanha Bay at the mouth of Langebaan Lagoon. Large fish factories and a naval base are polluting the area, and if left unchecked, will ultimately affect the fine balance of this ecosystem.

St Lucia

Lake St Lucia is the largest estuary in the country. It is a unique wetland endowed with a spectacular diversity of plant and animal life, with some 450 species of vertebrate fauna, of which at least 80 are listed as 'endangered' in the Red Data Book. However, as early as the 1950s, the State undertook a commercial afforestation programme on its eastern shores, which diminished the conservation value of the system. In the early 1970s, the government also granted prospecting leases to various bodies and companies, in conflict with the Ramsar Convention's designation of St Lucia as a wetland of international importance in 1986.

THREATS TO RIVERS

Pollution

Pollution is caused by the release of effluents from domestic as well as industrial sources into river courses. This affects the chemical content of and ultimately the biological life within the rivers.

One of the most severely polluted river systems in the country is the Jukskei-Crocodile River, which receives domestic and industrial effluents from the northern suburbs of Johannesburg. It has been estimated that as much as 50 per cent of the water flowing in the river originates from these effluents.

The result has been a severely degraded river habitat with poor water quality, as is evident by extensive environmental problems in the Hartbeespoort Dam, which receives this water. The dam has experienced massive blooms of the toxic blue-green alga (Microcystis aeruginosa), floating infestations of the alien water hyacinth, (Eichhornia crassipes), and occasional large fish kills.

Water flow and habitat degradation

It is estimated that all of South Africa's utilisable surface run-off has been impounded, resulting in less water flowing freely within river channels. This negatively affects the ability of these aquatic ecosystems to support a balanced community of organisms comparable to that of the natural habitat, in that it is detrimental to breeding and life-cycle habitats of aquatic organisms such as invertebrates, fish, plants and amphibians, and may prove insufficient as a water supply for wildlife, restricting the vegetation that borders the river. Additionally, evaporation and evapotranspiration will have a greater negative impact on the ecosystem; water quality will deteriorate, and sediment retention and obstruction by debris will increase.

Invasive alien species

There are at least 49 species of aquatic animals in South Africa that are considered to be alien. Twenty-three of these are invasive, and include trout and black bass, which have been introduced – much to the detriment of indigenous fish – throughout many river systems in South Africa as angling species.

Numerous aquatic plant species too have invaded river systems, causing blockages, and altering water flow patterns, decreasing oxygenation, reducing light intensity and providing breeding sites for disease vectors (for instance bilharzia).

Water hyacinth, kariba weed (Salvinia molesta), and parrot's feather (Myriophyllum aquaticum) are all invasive plant species, and are all present in the Orange-Vaal River system. Because of the highly regulated management of the system – which includes reservoirs, interbasin transfers, a system of weirs and reverse flows – these invasives have, in certain stretches, caused major management problems.

ABOVE Basking on a rock, a terrapin displays its webbed feet – an adaptation to aquatic living. Unlike tortoises, terrapins withdraw their heads by bending their necks.

The system has also been affected by decreased water flows from the Mkuze River in the north and the Mfolozi in the south caused by increased abstraction for agricultural and domestic use. Fresh water inputs to this lake are critical as hypersaline conditions are a threat to the wildlife of this wetland. Recently a decision was taken by the South African government that mining should not be allowed in this area.

Pongola flood plain

The Pongola flood plain is located in the most extensive coastal plain in the high rainfall area of South Africa, the Maputaland Plain. It is the only major flood plain incorporating a series of pans and is unique in South Africa. It has some interesting ecological aspects, such as the sand forest on the western boundary. This is a unique vegetation type that is fast disappearing due to subsistence farming. It is also the southern distribution limit of several tropical fish, and is an important winter feeding ground for large numbers of waterbirds.

The natural beauty of the flood plain, together with its many rare species, makes it one of the most aesthetically pleasing and interesting wetland areas in South Africa. As water resources have become scarcer, the flood plain has been severely threatened by regulation in the form of reservoirs and interbasin transfers, which dampens the natural variation in flow (low flows will have more water and high flows will have less). Thus, the Pongola River will be less likely to flood and the whole nature of the ecosystem will be changed, and the flood plain degraded. Other threats to the system include large-scale agricultural developments and subsistence farming.

ABOVE A water leguaan or monitor, swims in a savanna stream. Water leguaans are particularly partial to crocodile eggs.

ABOVE A brilliantly coloured purple gallinule stalks through a Highveld marsh, seeking out one of the aquatic plants or small animals on which it feeds.

Kosi Bay

The Kosi Bay system, in northern KwaZulu-Natal, consists of a series of interconnected estuarine lakes, entering the Indian Ocean five kilometres from the Mozambique border. The system constitutes an important wetland in terms of its diversity of life and unspoiled nature.

One of the special features of Kosi Bay is its mangrove forest. Mangroves are the only trees adapted to living in salty tidal waters and are ideal estuarine organisms. They shed large quantities leaves, which act as a food source for smaller organisms, and add to the detritus in the estuary. They also have a tremendous capacity for trapping silt, which stabilises the mudbanks, at the same time cleansing the water.

Unfortunately, closure of the estuary mouth due to decreased fresh water flows as a result of upstream water abstraction and use, has all but wiped out the mangrove forest.

Wilderness Lakes

The Wilderness Lakes, near Knysna, are three interconnected estuarine lakes: Eilandvlei, Langvlei and Rondevlei.

The lakes within the system exhibit varying degrees of salinity, depending on whether the mouth to the sea is open or not, and their distance from the mouth.

All of these lakes support dense growths of submerged and emergent aquatic plants, which form the basis of the food web in the system. They are essential nursery habitats for marine fish species. Furthermore, the lakes are important for ecotourism and recreation in the area, and their utilisation for these purposes will steadily increase.

ABOVE Having sighted a fish from the vantage point of a tall riverine tree, an African fish eagle swoops down for the kill.

Agricultural and land-use changes in the catchment are of concern in the long term, particularly as decreased water flow and increased sediment loads will increase the chances of siltation. In other words, if the water flow is decreased then topsoil washed into the system by rains wouldn't be flushed out, causing the lake to become more silted and shallow, and so unable to break through to the sea.

Kruger National Park rivers

A highly sensitive issue is water allocation to the rivers flowing through the Kruger National Park, South Africa's largest tourist attraction. There are six rivers that run through the Kruger: Levuvhu, Shingwedzi, Olifants, Letaba, Sabie and Crocodile. The park is situated at the lower end of the catchment areas, and is reliant on run-off from outside the conservation area to ensure ecological maintenance of the rivers. Development and water usage in the upper catchments of these rivers have changed the flow regime of some of them from perennial to a sporadic seasonal flow (for instance the Letaba and Levhuvhu rivers). This has been detrimental to the ecosystem, and has placed pressure on park authorities to provide alternate water supplies for the animals.

Of the Kruger Park rivers the Sabie is considered to have the highest conservation status. It supports a diverse riverine fauna, as well as a dense riparian forest. However, there are plans to regulate this river further, which, if implemented, could severely degrade the system, and may even cause the Sabie to dry up in the dry seasons.

Orange-Vaal river system

The Orange-Vaal river system is the largest river system in South Africa, its catchment area covering over 50 per cent of the country. The Orange River itself has a total length of 1 950 kilometres. It receives most of its run-off from the wetter eastern side of the subcontinent, and passes through the southern Free State and the arid Northern Cape to its mouth on the Atlantic Ocean.

Prior to any developments, especially those extracting water from the Vaal River, the natural run-off from this catchment was greater than 14 per cent of the total run-off of all the country's rivers. The amount of water currently reaching the Orange River Mouth at Alexander Bay (a Ramsar site) is 60 per cent of the natural run-off. This has severely threatened the unique salt marshes and wetland habitat of migratory and resident birds.

The decrease in the flow has been caused by regulation and extraction for industry in the Gauteng region, and for irrigation purposes further down the river. Because of the utilisation of the water flowing down the Vaal river, there is little or no natural Vaal water reaching the confluence with the Orange River.

The demand for water from the Vaal far outweighs the amount available in the system, creating the need to transfer water from the Lesotho Highlands. This transfer means that less water flows down the Orange River, exacerbating problems encountered below the Vaal-Orange confluence.

ABOVE *A bull elephant in the Shingwedzi River. An elephant drinks about 160 litres of water a day.*

ABOVE *The barbel, or catfish has an air-breathing organ situated above its gills, which enables it to live in very muddy water with a low oxygen content.*

ABOVE Displaying its horrific, interlocking teeth, a Nile crocodile lies in wait for a passing fish in the rapids of a swollen river.

WETLANDS: THREATS AND CONSERVATION

Wetland areas constitute some of the most threatened habitats in South Africa. Loss of wetland areas in this country has been brought about through human development activities such as channelisation, drainage, crop production, effluent disposal and water abstraction. Wetlands are often associated with the transmission of disease (such as malaria). Sadly, and even unbelievably, on these grounds alone, some have been filled in and reclaimed. This trend has been exacerbated by the fact that many wetlands are privately owned. Often the richness of wetland areas is enough reason for farmers to use them as agricultural land. Other threats include residential development (for instance, Marina da Gama in Cape Town).

While focus has been directed at larger wetlands 'of international importance', there is currently a lack of a conservation ethic regarding smaller wetlands, especially those on private land. Most of the wetland areas that are protected under the Ramsar convention are large – including Barbers Pan, Blesbokspruit, De Hoop Vlei, De Mond State Forest, the St Lucia system, turtle beaches and coral reefs of Tongaland (northern KwaZulu-Natal), Langebaan Lagoon, Wilderness Lakes, Verlorenvlei, the Kosi Bay system, Lake Sibaya, Natal Drakensberg Parks, Ndumo Game Reserve, Seekoeivlei, and the Orange River Mouth.

A smaller system also designated as a Ramsar site is Nylsvlei, which is the flood plain of the Nyl River that runs through the bushveld region of the Northern Province.

Although small, the Nylsvlei flood plain is of extraordinary importance for the maintenance of biological diversity. For many years at a time, it is just an expanse of dry grass. However, in years of high rainfall, it floods and becomes the most important South African breeding site of many uncommon and rare waterbird species. Creating awareness among landowners of the importance of such a wetland is a major conservation priority in South Africa, and would go a long way towards conserving the smaller wetland areas of this country.

Great Escarpment

Wayne S Matthews and George J Bredenkamp

Majestic peaks and cliffs, rolling grasslands with an extraordinary high biodiversity and endemism, patches of indigenous forest, swirling mists and abundant rains in summer, biting frost and even snow in winter – these images characterize the Great Escarpment. Described as a continuous 'necklace' of mountains and hills that separates the high-altitude interior plateau of South Africa from the narrow coastal plain, the Great Escarpment extends from the Western Cape, through the Eastern Cape, KwaZulu-Natal, Lesotho, Swaziland and Mpumalanga all the way up to the Northern Province, covering an incredible distance of more than 1 000 kilometres.

Escarpment areas constitute the highest altitude areas in South Africa, and in the KwaZulu-Natal Drakensberg areas, regular snowfalls are recorded during winter. The lower-altitude areas of the Mpumalanga and Northern Province escarpments generally tend to be warmer. Mean annual rainfall in most Escarpment areas exceeds 1 000 millimetres, and can be over 2 000 millimetres along the crests of peaks and scarps. Along the Mpumalanga and Northern Province escarpment there is a pronounced decrease of rainfall away from the crests on the leeward slopes. This results in rainfall shadow areas, such as the Blyde River Canyon and other areas west of the Escarpment crests, for example at the Ohrigstad Valley and The Downs. Rainfall in these areas is only about 600 millimetres a year.

The Escarpment continues across the borders of South Africa, northwards and eastwards into the continent. High altitude areas of the Escarpment form island-like centres of similar climate and vegetation throughout eastern Africa. Well-known examples are the eastern highlands of Zimbabwe (Chimanimani and Inyanga mountains), and Mount Mulanje and the Nyika plateau of Malawi. These 'archipelago' areas are classified as Afro-montane and/or Afro-alpine areas.

ORIGIN AND GEOLOGY

The Great Escarpment is arguably the single most important geomorphic feature of southern Africa. The present-day Escarpment, which in some areas lie more than 200 kilometres inland of the original continental

ABOVE As evening falls, a storm brews against the high mountain walls of the Drakensberg. In summer, the Berg is lashed by violent storms in three out of every four days.

margin, had its origin in the Gondwana break-up, which occurred approximately 200 million years ago. The complex mountain topography that we see today is the result of the many erosion cycles that followed the different geomorphic events.

The Gondwana break-up was followed by a long static period, during which weathering of these areas took place. This erosion removed about 500 to 700 metres of bed rock, and during this period the Escarpment receded, in places by some 100 kilometres from the coasts.

This was followed by an episodic event of continental uplift (150 to 300 metres), followed by a further static period except for weathering. The receding of the Escarpment during this period was limited, compared to the period after the Gondwana breakup.

The next episodic event was the one that made the Great Escarpment regions what they are today. An uplift of 600 to 900 metres took place. This rejuvenated rivers and resulted in the formation of deep river valleys and gorges. This too was followed by a static period, except for erosion cycles, which carved the landscape into what we know it as today; and this process still continues.

The Great Escarpment generally consists of sedimentary rocks that date back to the Gondwana break-up, The greater portion of the Escarpment is made up of sedimentary rocks such as sandstone and mudstone. Deep layers of various kinds of sandstone make up the spectacular sandstone cliffs in the eastern Free State, Lesotho, KwaZulu-Natal and Eastern Cape Drakensberg.

The Black Reef formation, which caps most of the Mpumalanga and Northern Province escarpment, is represented by a very clean quartzitic sandstone. Quartz is a very hard mineral, and is resistant to weathering, resulting in the persistent mountain peaks of this area. In the KwaZulu-Natal Drakensberg areas, however, the peaks are formed by basalts, a type of igneous lava rock formation. At the time of the Gondwana

ABOVE A mountain stream spills over an actively building tufa waterfall in the Blyde River Canyon.

break-up, the basaltic lava flowed from fissures that opened up in the area of the present-day Lesotho, and covered the underlying sedimentary rock formations. The thickness of the basalt layer varied from a few meters to over a 1 000 metres. This basalt forms the peaks and cliffs of the KwaZulu-Natal Drakensberg as we know it today.

An interesting rock formation of the Mpumalanga and Northern Province Escarpment is dolomite, a chemically based rock type that is soft and prone to intense weathering. Thus in these areas, caves and other related features are to be found, also known as a karst topography. The Sudwala and Echo caves are the best known of these.

Two other interesting characteristics of dolomite, which can be seen in the Escarpment, are olifantsklip ('elephant rock') and tufa.

Olifantsklip – so named because weathering has resulted in the exposed surface of the rock being similar to that of an elephant's hide – is the name given to the dolomite outcrops found in these areas.

Tufa is a rock-like feature formed by running water and under specific conditions, in dolomitic areas.

Dolomite is rich in calcium-carbonate, and weathering results in calcium-carbonate being dissolved into the water of rivers and streams. Under specific conditions and as a result of evaporation, algae and bacteria respiration activities in the rivers and streams, the calcium-carbonate is redeposited, forming rock-like features called tufa. This redepositing process results in the 'building up' of the 'rock' base of waterfalls, which is contrary to the normal weathering process of a waterfall – that is, cutting back of the rock base.

One of the biggest tufa waterfalls – and one which is still actively 'building' – is the Kadishi Tufa Falls, just below the Blydepoort resort, where the Kadishi stream enters the Blyde River Canyon. There are many remnant tufa formations to be seen in the dolomitic areas of the Mpumalanga and Northern Province Escarpment.

ABOVE Mutual grooming is an important form of social bonding in chacma baboons. Supremely adaptable, baboons are common in the mountains of the Escarpment.

ABOVE RIGHT An enormous bearded vulture glides effortlessly above the high plateau of the Drakensberg. Bones constitute a large proportion of its diet.

BELOW The striking orange-breasted rockjumper is an Escarpment endemic.

HABITATS AND ECOLOGICAL ZONES

The complex topography of the Great Escarpment creates a variety of distinct local habitats and zones. These localised areas are determined by variation in factors such as geology, slope, the aspect, soil depth and drainage pattern. The overriding factors, however, are rainfall – which provides accessible moisture for plants, and altitude – resulting in temperature zones. Fire is also an important ecological factor.

Three broad belts of different vegetation or habitat types (depicted as altitudinal zones) have been identified in the Great Escarpment areas.

The montane belt

The montane belt habitat type extends from an altitude of some 1 350 to 1 900 metres, and represents the relatively warm, wet zone of the Great Escarpment.

The vegetation of this belt is mainly represented by grassland on the rolling foothills, interspersed with many, isolated, tall and short forest patches in the sheltered kloofs and narrow valleys. These grasslands are represented by the northeastern montane grassland of the Northern Province, Mpumalanga and KwaZulu-Natal, and southeastern montane grassland of the Eastern Cape.

The subalpine belt

The subalpine belt, which extends from an altitude of 1 900 to 2 500 metres, represents Afro-montane grassland, and is a cool, wet zone.

This zone is also dominated by grassland, but a scrubland of fynbos is conspicuously present on the peak areas. Elements of the Cape Floral Kingdom found in this belt include plants such as *Erica, Philipia, Cliffortia, Passerina* and *Protea*.

ABOVE *Enormous layers of various kinds of sandstone form spectacular cliffs in the foothills of the Drakensberg. Portrayed here is a magnificent example in the Golden Gate Highlands National Park in the eastern Free State.*

The alpine belt

The alpine belt extends from 2 500 to above 3 000 metres, and represents alpine grassland and heathlands in the high, cold areas that regularly receive snow during the winter months. The environmental conditions are harsh, and these areas are dominated by scrubland/ heathlands. Fauna and flora are adapted to cope with these harsh conditions. The high altitude, marshy bogs of Lesotho, with its high incidence of endemic plant species, is one of the most interesting, limited and endangered habitats of the Escarpment area.

VEGETATION – BIODIVERSITY AND ENDEMISM

It was originally thought that the montane belt grassland areas of the Escarpment were dominated by forests, and that frequent burning of these areas by man had induced subclimax grassland landscapes with

the forests taking refuge in the gorges and rocky areas that were inaccessible to fire. Recent research, however, indicates that the grasslands were probably the original, dominant vegetation type in these areas. It has also been shown that 'natural' fires must have occurred in these montane grassland systems, long before man inhabited these areas, as the grasslands are adapted to burn annually or even biannually. The high biodiversity and degree of endemism recorded from these grassland areas is also indicative of the age and uniqueness of the grassland. While forests show a relative uniformity of species composition throughout their distribution range in Africa, grasslands show high levels of endemism, and a species-rich herbaceous flora.

In the KwaZulu-Natal Drakensberg, 39 per cent of the daisy family (Asteraceae) are local endemics. This region supports a total of approximately 1 400 plant species. The Mpumalanga and Northern Province escarpment, covering a larger area, has a total of some

1 600 plant species, of which 113 are endemic, with the Asteraceae also being one of the prominent endemic plant families. In the case of the Mpumalanga and Northern Province escarpments, the genus *Helichrysum* (everlastings) is the most prolific producer of endemic species.

An interesting example is *H. mariepscopicum*, named after the mountain peak Mariepskop, to which it is endemic.

The only species of indigenous bamboo (*Thamnocalamus tessellatus*) in South Africa, is found in the KwaZulu-Natal Drakensberg. This species, occurring on the stream banks and rocky areas in the montane belt, is endemic to the Escarpment area and the Lesotho Highlands.

Species with disjunct distributions include *Moraea muddi*, which is found on Mariepskop and in the Chimanimani Mountains of Zimbabwe, and on the high-lying areas of Malawi; and *Helichrysum swynnertonii*, which is found on Mariepskop and then again as far north as Mount Kilimanjaro.

ABOVE FROM LEFT TO RIGHT Crocosmia paniculata *grow in large colonies in moist grassland in the Escarpment region; New leaves of an ancient cycad –* Encephalartos transvenosus; Protea laetans *occurs in a single stand of several thousand trees on the edge of the Blyde River Canyon; Delicate everlastings (*Helichrysum *sp.) near Pilgrim's Rest, sway gently in the breeze, and fill the air with a sweet fragrance.*

Streptocarpus decipiens has only been collected twice – on Mariepskop and on the neighbouring Hebron Mountain.

The beautiful *Haemanthus pauculifolius*, which was only discovered in 1988, is known from only two localities – one in the Blyde River Canyon, which overlooks the Lowveld, and is situated in the Mpumalanga and Northern Province areas – and the other in the mountains near Barberton.

WILDLIFE – BIODIVERSITY AND ENDEMISM

In the upper reaches of the Treur River, only a narrow stream at this stage in the Mpumalanga section of the Escarpment, the river forms an impassable waterfall into what is known as the Christmas Pool.

This waterfall is the saviour of the Treur River barb (*Barbus treurensis*), a rare fish species endemic to the area. The barb occurs above the falls, but below it the fish has become extinct, due to

---

PEAKS AND FALLS

*T*he highest peak areas of the Escarpment, as well as those with the most spectacular proportions, are found in the KwaZulu-Natal Drakensberg. Here the Escarpment forms vertical rock walls, many of which can be sheer drops of more than 500 metres. These mountain landscapes are extremely rugged and vary in altitude from 762 to 3 483 metres. The highest point in the KwaZulu-Natal Drakensberg is Thabana-Ntlenyana (meaning the 'beautiful little mountain') at an altitude of 3 483 metres – this is also one of the highest points in southern Africa. Other well-known high peaks are Injasuti at 3 409 metres and Champagne Castle (Thaba Botlolo – the 'Bottle Mountain') at 3 377 metres.

The Mpumalanga and Northern Province escarpments do not house the spectacularly high peaks that the KwaZulu-Natal Drakensberg does. The altitude of the mountains in these provinces varies from 500 to 2 284 metres, and the highest peak – at 2 284 metres – is Mount Anderson (between the towns Sabie and Lydenburg). Other prominent northern peaks are Mauchberg (2 115 metres) and Iron Crown (2 126 metres).

Some of the lower, but nonetheless spectacular free-standing peaks are Serala (2 050 metres) in the Wolkberg Wilderness Area, Mariepskop (1 944 metres) at Blyde River Canyon, and the well-known God's Window (1 730 metres), which overlooks the Lowveld.

One of the most spectacular views in this region is that from Serala (which means 'plateau'), overlooking a very narrow ravine. The ravine is covered by dense indigenous forest, and at the entrance to the ravine, the Motlhake Semeetse (the 'river of light') waterfall is found. This ravine drops in altitude by an astonishing 1 365 metres over a distance of only four kilometres. Peaks of the Blyde River Canyon are as spectacular, some dropping 1 344 metres over a distance of five kilometres.

Due to the high rainfall, the Escarpment is one of the main catchment areas in southern Africa, and a main feature is the high incidence of sponges, marshes, streams and rivers.

A number of southern Africa's major rivers and their tributaries have their sources in the Escarpment region. This abundance of water in the rugged, complex topography of the mountains results in many drainage lines with beautiful, scenic waterfalls. The Tugela Falls in KwaZulu-Natal Drakensberg's Royal Natal National Park, is South Africa's highest water-fall, and is one of the highest in the world. The water drops a total of 850 metres in five leaps, against the dramatic rock wall of the Amphitheatre. The gorge beneath the falls is a spectacular sight to behold.

In Mpumalanga and the Northern Province some of the best known waterfalls are Mac Mac, Berlin and Lisbon.

ABOVE The spectacular Blyde River Canyon in Mpumalanga features a drop of approximately 1 344 metres within five kilometres.
BELOW The dream-like Bridal Veil falls near Sabie.

competition downstream with the exotic trout. Trout, a game fish, has been introduced for sport-angling (fly-fishing) into many of the clear, cold water streams found throughout the Escarpment areas. The barb was almost certainly saved from extinction by this waterfall, as trout cannot bridge this major obstacle to colonise the river above the falls.

The golden mole (*Amblysomnus gunningi*), and four species of reptiles are also endemic to this region. Of the reptile species one was only recently discovered and is still to be scientifically described. Another – Eastwood's long-tailed seps (*Tetradactylus eastwoodae*) – a small, snake-like plated lizard, has not been seen since its original scientific description in 1913, from the woodbush forests east of Tzaneen in the Northern Province. Unfortunately, the habitat of this rare seps species, in the vicinity of its original locality, has been destroyed by pine plantations.

There are also seven species and several subspecies of butterflies endemic to the Mpumalanga and Northern Province Escarpment,

CONSERVATION

*T*he larger conservation areas in the Mpumalanga and Northern Province escarpment are the Blyde River Canyon Nature Reserve, Wolkberg Wilderness Area and the Lekgalameetse Nature Reserve. There are also a few smaller government and private reserves in these Escarpment areas.

Blyde River Canyon Nature Reserve is famous for its scenery, with some outstanding topographic features such as The Three Rondawels, Pinnacle Rock, Mariepskop peak, God's Window, Bourke's Luck Potholes and many waterfalls, including the Kadishi Tufa Falls.

The Wolkberg Wilderness Area offers spectacular mountain scenery of forested gorges, peaks and deep ravines – a hiker's paradise.

The KwaZulu-Natal Drakensberg and the high Lesotho plateau run along approximately 250 kilometres of KwaZulu-Natal's western border. This area represents large, undeveloped tracts of land of unparalleled beauty.

One of the largest reserves or wilderness areas of this region is the Giant's Castle Game Reserve, which is famous for it's Bushman (San) rock art. The Escarpment of the Giant's Castle Game Reserve faces south, ensuring a longer snow-cover than is found anywhere else in the magnificent Drakensberg range.

One of the best-known Drakensberg reserves is the Royal Natal National Park. The dramatic rock wall known as the Amphitheatre and one of the highest waterfalls in the world (Tugela Falls) can be seen in this reserve. The Tugela gorge below the falls is a spectacular sight.

Most of the Drakensberg areas are ideal for extended mountaineering, climbing and hiking trips.

ABOVE *The highest peak areas of the Escarpment, as well as those having the most spectacular proportions, are found in the KwaZulu-Natal Drakensberg. Here the Escarpment forms vertical rock walls, some of which are sheer drops of more than 500 metres.*

ABOVE RIGHT *In the Royal Natal National Park, the bold outline and stupendous proportions of the Sentinel peak are revealed in their full splendour.*

including the obscure *Charaxis marieps*, a dark brown to black-coloured butterfly found along the edge of the Escarpment.

Many interesting birds are associated with the Great Escarpment. Three of the most publicised and threatened bird species are found here, namely the blue swallow (*Hirundo atrocaerulea*), the wattled crane (*Grus carunculatus*) and the bearded vulture (*Gypaetus barbatus*), also known as a lammergeier.

Three southern African endemics largely confined to the Escarpment region are the orange-breasted rockjumper (*Chaetops aurantius*), yellow-breasted pipit (*Anthus chloris*), and the Drakensberg siskin (*Serinus symonsi*).

The Escarpment is of major significance for migratory birds, as they use it as a north–south flyway because of the uplift created by the topography.

Birds such as the white stork (*Ciconia ciconia*), and the steppe buzzard (*Buteo buteo*), as well as a variety of other, smaller raptors, can be seen using these flyways as they move northwards.

ABOVE *The Cape vulture, the most common vulture in the Drakensberg, has an enormous wingspan that enables it to soar effortlessly for hours on end.*

Grassland

George J Bredenkamp

For many people, grassland landscapes seem monotonous and dull, especially during winter when they are brown and frost-bitten, or black and fire-scorched. Even during the rainy season in summer, grassland is often dismissed as uninteresting. So often in nature, however, things are not always as they seem and although grassland has a general uniformity – short vegetation, about 30 centimetres to 1.5 metres tall and dominated by grasses – there is considerable variation in plant species composition, functional attributes of plant species, vegetation dynamics and productivity. A closer look may, therefore, not only reveal a wealth of interesting plants and colourful wild flowers, but also a wide range of grassland animals.

The diveristy of life forms within grasslands results from wide environmental variations within the biome. For example, altitude varies from sea level to more than 3 000 metres, topography varies from flat plains to the majestic Drakensberg range – including wet bottomlands, rocky slopes, and vast plateaux.

Summer marks the rainy season, but again variation within the biome is great with rainfall ranging from 400 to more than 1 200 millimetres a year. Temperature, too, varies from frost free to snow-bound in winter, and from generally temperate to almost tropical.

The extent of the grassland biome, which occupies about 333 943 square kilometres, or 26 per cent of South Africa, is mainly limited by climatic factors. It is distinguished from neighbouring biomes by the number of days with sufficient soil moisture for plant growth, the mean temperature of these days, and the mean temperature of days too dry for plant growth. Generally, grasslands are moister than karoo, drier than forest and cooler than savanna, mostly with frost during the winter.

The economic importance of the South African grassland region is enormous. The country's gold and coal mining industries are centred in the Highveld grassland of the Gauteng, Mpumalanga, North-West, KwaZulu-Natal and the northern Free State provinces.

The mining industry triggered urban and industrial development, resulting in the biggest cities with the highest human population densities in the country. Furthermore, the climatic conditions are ideal for agriculture, especially the production of maize and sunflower crops, and

ABOVE A hillside that was burned in winter is carpeted in fresh green grass in early summer. These cabbage trees were protected by the rocks surrounding their stems.

about 49 per cent of the grassland of the Highveld Agricultural Region has been ploughed. Grassland also produces quality grazing.

Recently, too, forestry has become a major land-user within the grassland biome, with pine and eucalypt plantations presently covering large areas of the higher rainfall, eastern plateau.

REGIONS AND VEGETATION TYPES

From the floristic variation over the east–west rainfall gradient, six major regions – comprising 14 grassland vegetation types – can be recognised.

Western region

This sandy, dry and hot region is characterised by species with Kalahari affinities, such as Lehmann's lovegrass (*Eragrostis lehmanniana*) and silky bushman grass (*Stipagrostis uniplumis*). Although rainfall is erratic, making this a high-risk area for agriculture, and despite its suitability for livestock farming due to the sweet nature of the grazing, large areas have been ploughed. The natural vegetation is often restricted to shallow or wind-blown soils and pans, and these are often overgrazed.

Central inland plateau region

The central inland plateau region is dominated by red grass (*Themeda triandra*). This grass outcompetes and overshadows many wild flower species, and the area is consequently low in diversity of plant species.

Other prominent grass species include spear grass (*Heteropogon contortus*), wire grass (*Elionurus muticus*), and narrow-leaved turpentine-grass (*Cymbopogon plurinodis*). The soils of this area are excellent for crops and they are mostly ploughed for maize cultivation.

Northern region

These grasslands – transitional to savanna – occur on a mosaic of exposed plains and sheltered, rocky hills. Variation in topography, geology and soil creates a variety of microhabitats, resulting in a very rich flora. Plains are often dominated by central inland plateau species, indicating affinities with the typical grassland, while the shallow rocky soils are dominated by sour grasses such as giant spear grass (*Trachypogon spicatus*), red autumn grass (*Schizachyrium sanguineum*), common russet grass, (*Loudetia simplex*) and Natal panicum (*Panicum natalensis*).

ABOVE *The huge wattled crane is very rare in South Africa. Small numbers occur in the grasslands of KwaZulu-Natal and the high-lying areas of Mpumalanga.*

This northern region is rich in beautiful wild flower species. Amongst those occurring are, for example, many everlastings (*Helichrysum* spp.) and other members of the daisy family (Asteraceae), acanthus family (Acanthaceae), mint family (Lamiaceae), and orchid family (Orchidaceae). A large number of these grasses and wild flowers are typical of the Drakenberg Afro-montane area. However, savanna species, especially sour bushveld trees such as common hook-thorn (*Acacia caffra*), mountain karree (*Rhus leptodictya*), velvet bushwillow (*Combretum molle*), and many more, occur in sheltered spots.

The plant species composition and species-richness clearly suggest that the vegetation of the Bankenveld, as this northern region was called by Acocks (see box on page 80), has a heterogeneous origin, with contributions from grassland, savanna and the Drakensberg.

Eastern inland plateau region
The eastern inland plateau region, just west of the Drakensberg range, is situated at a higher altitude than the central inland plateau. It is accordingly much cooler and has a higher rainfall. Here species such

as Ngongoni three awn (*Aristida junciformis*) and tough lovegrass (*Eragrostis plana*), and on extremely clayey, black soils, rolling grass (*Aristida bipartita*) and vlei bristlegrass (*Setaria incrassata*) are important constituents of the vegetation.

Eastern mountains and escarpment region
This region is typified by Afro-montane species such as golden velvet grass (*Eulalia villosa*), boat grass (*Monocymbium cereciiforme*), caterpillar grass (*Harpochloa falx*), and sickle grass (*Ctenium concinnum*). A large variety of wild flowers occur in this area. Its unique Afro-montane character, great biodiversity, high endemism and scenic beauty make this area of the Great Escarpment so important that a separate chapter is devoted to it (see pages 64–73).

Eastern lowland region
The grassland region to the east of the Drakensberg Escarpment is dominated by the tall common thatching grass (*Hyparrhenia hirta*). This type of vegetation is often evident on disturbed, previously ploughed or

ABOVE, FROM LEFT TO RIGHT The central inland plateau region of South Africa is dominated by red grass – a climax grass; Leonotis leonurus; Natal red-top, a pioneer grass.

heavily overgrazed sites, indicating a possible recent anthropogenous (human-induced) origin. The abundance of archaeological sites in this region substantiates this viewpoint.

VELD CONDITION

For all farmers and managers of grazing land, it is important to be able to evaluate the 'condition' of the veld. Condition refers to the general health of the grass layer, its potential to produce valuable fodder, and the veld's resistance to erosion.

Veld condition is often a function of plant species composition. Certain grass species, normally sweet grasses, are termed 'decreasers', and are abundant in veld that is in good condition, but become less so where the veld is over- or undergrazed.

Other species will increase when the veld is underutilised – these are known as 'Increaser I' species and are mostly sour grasses. A third group, the 'Increaser II species', increases when the veld is overgrazed.

Armed with this understanding, an overall assessment of the condition of the veld in any given area can easily be made. Veld dominated by Decreasers is obviously in a very good condition. If Increaser I species dominate, the veld is underutilised, but if Increaser II species are predominantly present the veld is overutilised and in a poor condition.

VEGETATION

Natural plant biodiversity in grassland is surprisingly high, with an estimated 3 378 plant species occuring in the core region. In terms of the number of plant species occurring in sample areas of 1 000 square metres, the grassland biome is richer than even the fynbos biome. Overall, however, and in terms of the estimated total amount of plant species per biome, the grassland biome lies third after the fynbos biome (which has an estimated 7 316 species) and the savanna (with an estimated 5 788 species).

In contrast to European grasslands that are considered as relatively young, man-made vegetation that replaced the forests, South African grasslands are thought to be very old. They were widespread more than 12 000 years ago and are probably not derived from forests through human activities. The most important evidence of this is from fossil pollen, and drier and cooler climatic conditions favouring grassland rather than forest during the last Glacial Period, which dates back as far as 18 000 years ago. The high levels of endemism in South African grassland species, as opposed to forest species, also indicate a long evolutionary history of the grasslands. In modern times, however, it seems that human practices, including the use of fire, do maintain the present grassland-forest interface and, in fact, enhance development of grassland at the expense of forest in the eastern mountain regions.

ABOVE *Black wildebeest – endemic to the plains of the South African interior, wade through the summer grasses below an ominous stormy sky.*

Sweet and sour grasses

Within the grassland biome, as within the bushveld, sweet and sour grasses occur, determining the suitability of the veld for grazing (see 'Bushveld' page 28 for a fuller explanation of these terms).

Sweet veld normally occurs in the drier, warmer areas, with less than 500 millimetres of rainfall, while sour veld is predominant in the cooler, high rainfall areas (more than 625 millimetres). In areas of intermediate climate a mixed veld occurs. With higher rainfall, the vegetation is more productive but the soil is easily leached of nutrients and it becomes more acid. Furthermore, during cold, frosty winters nutrients are translocated from the dying leaves to underground parts where they are stored, to be used again in the following spring for the resprouting of the grass plant. This is also an adaptation to mitigate the influence of fire, which is characteristically part of the sour veld ecosystem.

Sweet veld is very susceptible to overgrazing, especially during the growing season, but is fortunately able to recover quickly, if managed well, after good rains. Sour veld produces good grazing during the growing season. Although it has a resilience against overgrazing, it recovers very slowly after being mismanaged. In all veld types, but especially in mixed veld, a proper grazing management strategy will prevent the overutilisation of sweet grass, resulting souring of the veld, and consequently the lowering of the grazing capacity of the area.

Karoo invasion

Acocks suggested that the karoo is expanding north and eastwards into the grassland biome at a rate of one to two kilometres a year. Various authors have attributed this expansion of the karoo to poor veld management, especially overgrazing by domestic livestock, which eliminates perennial grasses. It has been indicated that continuous grazing of the veld, especially during the summer growing season of the grasses, enhances the presence of karoo dwarf shrubs at the expense of perennial grasses, while almost pure perennial grassland develops under protection during higher rainfall.

The southwestern boundary of the grassland biome interfaces with the Nama-karoo. This boundary coincides with a transitional zone of rainfall uncertainty, with grassland on the wetter, higher altitudes, and karoo on the drier, lower altitude side. This uncertainty of rainfall caused the development of a generalist flora, capable of tolerating these variations in climatic conditions. Recently it was suggested that the grassland-karoo interface shifts as a result of cyclic shifts in the seasonality and amount of the rainfall, with higher, spring-summer rains promoting grassland, and lower, autumn-winter rainfall.

Within this transitional zone, the distribution of grassland and karoo vegetation is also influenced by soil texture – with grassland occurring on the moister, sandy soils, and karoo vegetation on drier, clayey soils.

ABOVE, FROM LEFT TO RIGHT The brilliant red flowers of **Erythrina zeyheri** *constitute the mere tip of what may be described as an underground tree; The striking flower-head of* Brunsvigia radulosa *will, when dry, become a 'tumble-weed' that will be blown around in the wind; A dense stand of aloes (*Aloe marlothii*) graces a steep slope in the Suikerbosrand Nature Reserve near Heidelberg.*

Many vegetation studies in the western part of the grassland biome showed islands of karoo vegetation on dry, clayey soils within the boundaries of the grassland. These islands cannot be regarded as karoo encroachment into the grassland biome – they rather represent specialised, dry, karoo-like habitats within grassland vegetation.

It can be concluded that, although overgrazing does enhance change of grassland to karoo vegetation, annual variation in rainfall can be regarded as the primary driving force on vegetation dynamics in the grassland-karoo interface.

Bush encroachment and 'false grasslands'

To the north and the east, grassland often intergrades with savanna. In these regions woody species often invade grasslands, mostly as a result of reduced grass cover due to sustained heavy grazing by livestock. This phenomenon is called bush encroachment – a sure sign of veld mismanagement.

Acocks termed certain transitional zones between typical savanna and typical grassland, 'false grassland' types, for example the Bankenveld and the Pietersburg plateau.

He thought that the climax vegetation of these areas should have been savanna, but that they had been transformed into and maintained as grassland by fire. However, the fire regimes in the adjacent savanna and grassland vegetation systems are not different. This suggests that the difference between savanna and grassland should rather be sought in climatic conditions – grassland being much colder with frost in the non-growing season. This is mostly a result of altitude.

Grassland occurs on exposed, cold higher altitudes and savanna on lower lying plains or sheltered valleys or slopes at higher altitudes.

The important role of fire in both savanna and grassland is not denied – in fact, fire played a critical and determinant role in the development and maintenance of the flora, and consequently the fauna, of both these vegetation types.

Many wild flowers of both savanna and grassland will not, for example, produce flowers and consequently seeds for reproduction, if the vegetation was not burned the previous dry season.

ABOVE FROM LEFT TO RIGHT The endemic blesbok is a popular subject for game farming. In historic times, large herds of antelope and zebra roamed the central plains of South Africa. Today, vastly reduced numbers survive in small grassland reserves and on game farms; Eland, largest of the African antelopes, also used to occur widely in grassland habitats. *BELOW* A summer, noonday sky above the grasslands.

Furthermore, the seeds of many plant species (woody and herbaceous), will only germinate after a veld fire. In fact, the growth form of grasses indicates a strong adaptation to defoliation, either by grazing or by fire. The renewal buds of the great majority of grass species are situated at or below the soil surface, well protected against grazing and fire.

In addition, most non-grass herbaceous species such as bulbs (grass lily – *Crinum graminicola*, poison bulb – *Boophane disticha*), rhizomes (orchids) and tubers (elephant's root – *Elephantorrhiza elephantina*, and *Erythrina zeyheri*), have well-developed underground storage organs from where they regrow after a fire.

In the short term, however, fire and grazing may affect the ratio of woody versus grass species cover. Overgrazing often enhances and fire oppresses the development of a woody component in transitional areas.

WILDLIFE

Grassland is fodder for many animals, and can sustain large herds of black wildebeest (*Connochaetus gnou*), Burchell's zebra (*Equus burchelli*), blesbok (*Damaliscus dorcas phillipsi*) and springbok (*Antidorcas marsupialis*). However, the grasslands have suffered the same fate as the bushveld: the huge migratory herds that once roamed these areas have disappeared. Fortunately, smaller numbers of all the grassland game species can still be found in a network of small reserves and game farms scattered throughout the biome. The black wildebeest was nearly extinct during the first half of this century, but due to conservation measures it is now abundantly present. Of the smaller mammals, the oribi (*Ourebia*

ourebi), rough-haired (*Chrysospalax villosus*) and the hottentot (*Amblysomus hottentotus*) golden moles are endemic to grassland.

Of the 35 bird species endemic to South Africa, 10 are restricted to the grassland biome. These are the bald ibis (*Geronticus calvus*), blue korhaan (*Eupodotis caerulescens*), Rudd's lark (*Heteromirafra ruddi*), buff-streaked chat (*Oenanthe bifasciata*), orange-breasted rockjumper (*Chaetops aurantius*), Drakensberg prinia (*Prinia hypoxantha*), mountain pipit (*Anthus hoeschi*), yellow-breasted pipit (*A. chloris*), and Drakensberg siskin (*Serinus symonsi*).

ABOVE *The ornate crowned crane forages in grassland, but builds its nest in marshes. It is regarded as a sacred bird by some tribal peoples.*

ABOVE *Numbers of the blue crane, national bird of South Africa, have declined alarmingly in grassland regions.*

ABOVE *In summer-time, the male long-tailed widow is a striking sight.*

Some 15 other South African endemics are species typical of, but not restricted to the grassland biome. This group includes the grey-wing francolin (*Francolinus africanus*), blue crane (*Anthropoides paradisea*), ground woodpecker (*Geocolaptus olivaceus*), sentinel rock thrush (*Monticola explorator*), rock pipit (*Anthus crenatus*), and pied starling (*Spreo bicolor*).

The importance of the grassland biome for the conservation of the endemic birds of South Africa should be clear. The South African Red Data Book for Birds includes 102 species. Of these, 49 utilise dry or wet grassland or waterbodies. This strongly suggests that grasslands and

THREATS AND CONSERVATION

*T*he grassland biome contains some of the most threatened vege-tation types in South Africa. It is estimated that 60 to 80 per cent of South African grasslands have already been irreversibly transformed by agriculture, forestry, urban and industrial development and mining. An alarmingly low two per cent of the remaining pockets of pristine grasslands – areas of surprisingly high plant and animal diversity – are formally under conservation in 142 publicly owned nature reserves. On the positive side, by correlation of the geographic distribution of the 3 378 plant species found in the grassland biome, and the distribution of these nature reserves, it is estimated that 78 per cent of these species are indeed represented in conservation areas.

A reason for concern is the extensive commercial afforestation over large areas of land in the high rainfall eastern Escarpment area, a region of exceptionally high biodiversity, which contains 30 per cent of the endemic and rare plant species of the former Transvaal Province.

Some of the more prominent conservation areas within the grass-land biome include the Golden Gate Highlands National Park, Sterkfontein Dam Nature Reserve and Willem Pretorius Nature Reserve in the Free State, Suikerbosrand Nature Reserve in Gauteng, parts of the Blyde River Canyon Nature Reserve and Songimvelo Nature Reserve in Mpumalanga, the Drakensberg reserves and wilderness areas and Itala Game Reserve in KwaZulu-Natal, Boskop Dam Nature Reserve, Bloemhof Dam Nature Reserve and SA Lombard Nature Reserve in the North-West Province, and parts of the Mountain Zebra National Park in the Eastern Cape.

It is now too late to bring back the large migratory herds of grass-land herbivores. However, it is imperative that the existing reserve net-work be maintained and expanded to conserve viable populations of South Africa's unique grassland species. The first step is to alert the South African public to the fact that a hitherto disregarded heritage is slipping away. Warwick Tarboton, an eminent South African ornitholo-gist, expressed it succinctly:

'If ever a biome needed a champion, it is the grassland.'

ABOVE *The handsome jackal buzzard is a southern African endemic. Its name refers to its jackal-like call.*

BELOW RIGHT *The Steenkampsberg in Mpumalanga is an area of relatively unspoilt, high-altitude grassland. It is renowned for its wild flowers and crane-breeding efforts.*

wetlands of South Africa have been subjected to great ecological stress. With the present afforestation in the moist eastern grasslands, the blue swallow (*Hirundo atrocaerulea*) became an important vulnerable species.

Agriculture and forestry have destroyed large parts of the habitat of spectacular species such as the blue crane and especially the wattled crane (*Grus carunculatus*).

The giant sungazer lizard (*Cordylus giganteus*) is one of the strangest, yet most endearing inhabitants of the South African grasslands. These miniature 'dragons' live in colonies in holes in the ground. During the day they emerge from their burrows and point their heads towards the sky, as if worshipping the sun. They carry protective armour of very rough and spiny scales, giving them a truly prehistoric appearance. Their colonies are frequently situated on land with prime agricultural potential, with the result that entire colonies may be destroyed by ploughing.

Nama Karoo

↲ Wendy Lloyd

For many the name 'Karoo' conjures up impressions of endless, dreary brown plains, beaten

by a relentless sun, and mirages making a watery mockery of the arid horizons. But this is all just a

matter of perception, and if you take the time to better acquaint yourself with the Karoo's intangible

beauty, you would be pleasantly surprised. The Nama karoo is the second largest biome in South Africa. Its

plains of dwarf shrubs and grasses are dotted with characteristic koppies, forming a compelling

landscape, especially when the sun sets and the sky is lit with brilliant, indescribable hues.

Nights are inky black, and studded with a myriad tiny, shining stars.

The Nama karoo biome is essentially a grassy, dwarf shrubland, most of which lies between 1 000 and 1 400 metres above sea level. Eastwards, the ratio of grasses to shrubs increases progressively, until the Nama karoo eventually merges with the grassland biome. On the northern fringes – its interface with the savanna biome – the dwarf shrubland often has an overstorey of shrubs and trees. It does not have a unique or species-rich flora, with only 2 147 plant species, of which 386 (18 per cent) are endemic and 67 are threatened.

Extensive, flat to gently undulating plains, broken by familiar Karoo dolerite koppies, best describe the landscape. Mountainous areas in the biome include the Nuweveld Mountains in the vicinity of Beaufort West, and the Katberg sandstone range near Middelburg.

'Karoo' is the Khoi word for 'dry', and this aptly describes the Nama karoo biome, which is regarded as a semi-desert area because it receives less than 500 millimetres of rain a year. Precipitation is unpredictable, and sporadic. The mean annual rainfall ranges from 100 millimetres in the west, to 520 millimetres in the east, and occurs predominantly in the summer. Humidity is low. In the winter, the mean minimum monthly temperature can drop to below minus 9°C in places. In summer, the mean maximum monthly temperature can exceed 40°C.

GEOLOGICAL HISTORY AND PALAEONTOLOGY
The geological history of this biome gives an indication of the climate, habitats, ecosystems and biodiversity of the region in ancient times.

CONSERVATION

Less than one per cent of the Nama karoo biome is conserved, with the exception of the Orange River Nama karoo (1.47 per cent) and eastern mixed Nama karoo (1.08 per cent) The highest densities of threatened plant species have been recorded in the Steytlerville, Great Karoo and Noorsveld regions, but scientific plant specimens have generally been poorly collected throughout the biome as a whole.

The Karoo National Park at Beaufort West, Mountain Zebra National Park near Cradock, and Augrabies Falls National Park on the Orange River west of Kakamas, are all situated within the Nama karoo biome. Provincial nature reserves include Oviston, Doornkloof and Rolfontein nature reserves, all of which are situated along the Orange River and contain numerous bird and game populations. The dolerite pillars in the Valley of Desolation are special features of the Karoo Nature Reserve, which virtually surrounds the town of Graaff-Reinet. Rare plants include elephant's foot (Dioscorea elephantipes) and vingerpol (Euphorbia polycephala).

Anysberg Nature Reserve covers a transitional area between the Little Karoo and the Great Karoo. It is a centre of speciation of the genus Astroloba and Conophytum, and represents the most easterly distribution of a number of typical western Cape elements. Two Red Data Book lizards, one snake and numerous plant species, some locally endemic, occur in the areas. A number of local authority nature reserves, and the Platberg-Karoo Conservancy near the town of De Aar, are also represented within this biome.

The possibility of re-establishing presettlement animal communities and grazing patterns exists for only three reserves, each of which is larger than 15 000 hectares.

Threatened and sensitive habitats include riverine areas, pans and drainage systems, as well as localised red sand dunes and succulent plant habitats (e.g. specific calcrete, dorbank and quartz patches).

Conservation challenges include obtaining a predictive understanding of ecological processes that operate in this arid and semiarid region, improving management of the natural resources of the biome by preserving biodiversity and ensuring sustainable resource utilisation, and heightening awareness of the ecological effects of management practices by local farmers.

ABOVE The beautifully proportioned lanner falcon is a fearsome hunter of the skies. In arid areas it can be frequently seen ambushing birds coming down to waterholes.

The remarkable fossil record from this region is world famous, with a wealth of information on dinosaurs and other prehistoric mammal-like reptiles, revealing much evidence on the origin of mammals.

When travelling through the Karoo today, it is difficult to imagine that, in prehistoric times, most of this area was covered by a swamp or swamp-like forest and inhabited by dinosaurs, or that it was, at some stage, covered by glaciers!

The main geological layers covered by the Nama karoo are sediments of the Dwyka Formation, which is overlain by the Ecca and Beaufort groups, respectively. Dolerite intrusions occur scattered throughout the sandstones and shales of the Ecca and Beaufort groups.

The Dwyka Formation in northern Bushmanland has a maximum thickness of 250 metres, formed from debris that was deposited on land by glaciers approximately 300 million years ago.

These deposits sometimes rest on striated pavements, which indicate that the glaciers moved in a south and southwesterly direction from the icecap that formed over what is now Botswana, the Northern Cape and the North-West Province.

There is evidence, in the form of plant remains within the Dwyka tillites, that there were also unglaciated areas that supported vegetation. After this period of glaciation, a large shallow lake – deeper in the south than in the north – formed over the entire Nama karoo area. Evidence is provided by the beds of the Ecca Group, which vary in thickness from approximately 3 000 metres in the south to about 300 metres in the north. Beds of the Ecca Group in Bushmanland were formed by the deposit of material derived from higher-lying mountains in the west and northeast on large deltas which built up in the lake from about 280 to 240 million years ago. Fossil tree trunks found in sediments of the Ecca Group near Douglas provide evidence of heavily forested shorelines. Dry land on the deltas and suitable climate also made it possible for the first terrestrial reptiles to migrate into the basin.

Eventually these deltas filled the entire basin, and the beds of the Ecca Group were covered by river deposits of the Beaufort Group about 240 to 195 million years ago. Braided streams and meandering rivers flowed in from mountains to the southeast and southwest, where coarse-grained debris was deposited along their slopes.

In what is now northern Bushmanland and Gordonia, finer sediments were laid down by meandering streams on large flood plains. Arid to semiarid conditions prevailed during the deposition of the Beaufort beds, which is indicated by the presence of desert rose rocks (pseudomorphs), evidence of seasonal flash floods, few plant remains and the small fossilised *Glossopteris* (a fossil fern-like gymnospermous plant) leaves.

The different subenvironments that existed each contain their own characteristic suite of vertebrate remains that illustrate the preference the reptiles had for particular environments.

Fish (*Atherstonia*) flourished in some of the more permanent ponds, and together with large semiaquatic herbivorous reptiles (*Pareiasauria*), occupied the lakes of the central flood basin. Terrestrial forms, in particular mammal-like reptiles (*Therapsida*), were supported by the sparse, stunted vegetation (*Glossopteris* flora) on the banks of the river channels. Both herbivorous and carnivorous dinocephalia existed at that time, most of the herbivores being dicynodonts.

The climate in the Karoo basin became wetter at the end of the Permian Period (225 million years ago), during which time a change in the fauna also occurred. The dicynodont genus, *Lystrosaurus*, a semi-aquatic, dwarf hippopotamus-like animal that occupied the marshy swamplands, replaced the pareiasaurs and other dicynodont genera that were abundant during the drier period. The fossils preserved in the shales of the Beaufort Group represent one of the most complete and best preserved assemblages of terrestrial fossil vertebrates known. The period from 240 to 190 million years ago was particularly important because it saw the evolution of the first mammals (fossils of the mammal-like reptiles provided the link between primitive reptiles and the first true mammals).

ABOVE The dramatic quiver tree is characteristic of the rocky hills in the hot drainage basin of the Orange River. Its vernacular name alludes to the use of its bark by the Bushman (San) people to make quivers for their poison arrows.

ABOVE, FROM LEFT TO RIGHT The flowers of Hoodia gordonii *smell like rotting flesh – an adaptation to attract flies as pollinators; The klipspringer (meaning rock-jumper) is supremely adapted to rocky habitats, where it can evade most predators;* Euphorbia stellispina *is remarkably similar to American cacti.*

The Karoo dolerite sills and dykes are igneous rocks formed from 187 to 150 million years ago when molten rock intruded into the pre-existing rocks of the Ecca and Beaufort Groups. Dolerites form the characteristic Karoo koppies because they are generally more resistant to weathering than the sandstones and softer shales. The dolerite sills and dykes also play an important role in controlling the movement of underground water.

The tertiary surface calcrete, which is extensive on the Bushmanland Plateau, probably formed during a semiarid climate with summer rainfall at the end of the Miocene, about 12 million years ago, when there was a period of geomorphic stability.

Today the Nama karoo is drained primarily by the Orange River basin, although many of the water courses that feed it are seasonal. Panveld, with internal drainage basins, covers large parts of Bushmanland, and one of the unique physical features of the Nama karoo biome is the Grootvloer-Verneukpan complex, which is the largest pan system in South Africa. The Grootvloer system plays an important role during fish migrations, allowing certain species access to their breeding grounds in the upper reaches of the Sak River. It is the only link between the Orange and Sak river systems during periods of high summer rainfall when there may be an interchange of indigenous fish and other aquatic organisms.

The pans and drainage lines in the Nama karoo provide important habitats for certain fauna. During dry climatic cycles, the relatively wetter and more vegetated pans, pan fringes, and drainage lines may serve as migration routes for mammals. Grootvloer is also well known for its consistently high lark population, particularly the rarer small larks that are confined to Bushmanland and southern Namibia. Grootvloer occasionally floods, making it a rich habitat for the area, and, therefore, an important source for repopulating the surrounding areas.

BROWN LOCUST OUTBREAKS

*The eggs of the brown locust (*Locustana pardalina*) are not only drought-resistant, but remain dormant, accumulating in the soil over a number of seasons. These eggs have a high viability and hatch simultaneously when there are widespread rains following a drought.*

Swarming adults may form large egg beds, which are potentially able to produce over 250 million 'hoppers' per hectare. The main swarming area of the brown locust is the Nama karoo biome where outbreaks are relatively infrequent; relatively, because in previous centuries, locust irruptions lasted up to 13 years at a time, with quiet periods of about 11 years in-between. Natural predation and an improvement in chemical control measures have reduced the irruptions to periods of about two years, with quiet periods of about two years in-between.

*Locusts (eggs, nymphs and adults) provide a prey source for a variety of natural predators, including meerkats (*Suricata suricatta*) and bat-eared foxes (*Octocyon megalotis*). However, in order to effectively wipe out an irruption of locusts and the remaining 'flitters', these natural predators need to continually consume the locusts over a period of at least seven years! The 'flitters' survive chemical control operations and are able to build up to plague proportions within two to three years.*

Whether or not the eradication of locust outbreaks would be a good thing, is a controversial issue. For example, prior to domestic livestock fencing, numbers of indigenous herbivores would have been depleted at the end of a dry cycle – as a result of migration, starvation, natural mortality and predation. Under these circumstances, locusts were probably the most important herbivores in the biome. Further, locusts may play an ecologically signficant role by rapidly returning nutrients to the soil in the form of frass (excrement).

ABOVE The northern parts of the Nama karoo constitute some of the most arid areas in South Africa. However, in the rare event of good summer rains, grasses are more dominant here than in the southern parts of the biome.

VEGETATION TYPES

Six major vegetation types are recognised in the Nama karoo biome.

Bushmanland Nama karoo

Situated at an altitude of 900 metres in the most arid northwestern parts of the biome, this area records rainfall of only 50 to 200 millimetres a year. The vegetation is dominated by cauliflower ganna (*Salsola tuberculata*) and bushman grasses (*Stipagrostis obtusa* and *S. ciliata*).

Annuals are common, and together with geophytes comprise nearly 50 per cent of the plant species of the region.

Upper Nama karoo

This area occurs at altitudes of 1 050 to 1 700 metres. It also receives a very low rainfall – approximately 250 millimetres a year. This vegetation occurs more commonly on rocky and hilly areas, and is dominated by the dwarf shrubs kapokbush (*Eriocephalus ericoides*),

silverkaroo (*Plinthus karooicus*) and perdekaroo (*Rosenia humilis*). Grasses are rare, but after rains tassel bristlegrass (*Aristida congesta*) and Lehmann's lovegrass (*Eragrostis lehmanniana*) sometimes become prominent in the upper Nama karoo.

Orange River Nama karoo

As the name suggests, this area occurs in the hot, dry Orange River Basin, at altitudes of 250 to 350 metres. The rainfall is low, between 150 and 250 millimetres per year. The entire region is rocky, with a complex topography including many hills and slopes. Here drought-resistant succulent tree species such as the quiver tree (*Aloe dichotoma*) and bushman poison tree (*Euphorbia avasmontana*) predominate.

Tree species usually associated with the savanna biome, such as black thorn (*Acacia mellifera*) and shepherd's tree (*Boscia albitrunca*), occur on the plains. The aggressively encroaching threethorn shrub (*Rhigozum trichotomum*) may invade the plains vegetation here.

ABOVE Stripped bare by aeons of erosion, the geological layers of the Nama karoo lie exposed in the Karoo National Park.

Eastern mixed Nama karoo

The eastern mixed Nama karoo forms a transition to the grassland biome to the east of the Nama karoo. It receives a relatively high rainfall of 300 to 500 millimetres a year. Due to the rain, herbaceous vegetation cover is higher, and consequently this is the only Nama karoo area where fire plays a role in shaping the plant communities. Dwarf shrubs, for example bitterkaroo (*Chrysocoma tenuifolia*) and kapokbos are still dominant, but grassland species such as red grass (or rooigras) (*Themeda triandra*) often dominate the landscape after good summer rains.

Great Nama karoo

This area lies in the rain shadow of the Great Escarpment and the Swartberg, and receives a rainfall of only 150 to 250 millimetres a year. The vegetation is dominated by a great variety of dwarf shrubs, such as anchor karoo (*Pentzia incana*), wild pomegranate (*Rhigozum obovatum*) and ghombos (*Felicia filifolia*). Grasses are scanty.

Central lower Nama karoo

Situated to the east of the great Nama karoo, the central lower Nama karoo shares many dwarf shrub species with that region. However, this region has a considerably greater incidence of succulent plants. The area receives a mix of summer and winter rainfall.

VEGETATION – SURVIVAL STRATEGIES

Vegetation distribution patterns are linked to variations in geology and associated soils, and a distinction exists between plant communities requiring moister soils, and those requiring higher nutrient-status soils. Vegetation is also adapted to saline or calcareous soil conditions, where the incidence of non-succulent dwarf shrubs is higher, and is virtually absent on saline soils, where succulent-leaved dwarf shrubs and succulents predominate. Some plants survive because they are able to store water in their thick leaves or root systems, and others may become deciduous in response to the high frequency of drought-like conditions.

An adaptation shown by many plants is that of camouflage and mimicry. For example, kalkvygie (*Titanopsis schwantesii*) has whitish tubercles that resemble the calcrete nodules on which it grows, and the white haasbos (*Anacampseros papyracea*) grows on patches of white quartz pebbles. Various *Lithops* species are known as 'flowering stones', or stone plants because they look like the pebbles around them, while the dotted leaves of quaggakos (*Pleiospilos bolusii*) and mimicry plants (*Pleiospilos simulans*), are also stone-like in appearance.

In this dry, low-production ecosystem, fire is not an important feature. Exceptions are the wetter northeastern and mountainous parts where fuel-loads are adequate in high rainfall seasons, and wildfires may be started by lightning strikes.

WILDLIFE

The Nama karoo supports 131 desert vertebrates. One amphibian, nine reptile, five mammal and two bird species are endemic to the biome. Nama karoo animals are often well adapted to their dry, hostile environments. They are also well camouflaged in rocky and sandy habitats, particularly lizards, geckos and snakes, whose body colour and patterns enable them to blend in with their surroundings.

Numerous insects, including grasshoppers and locusts, resemble dry twigs or leaves, and ground-dwelling birds, such as the Namaqua sandgrouse (*Pterocles namaqua*), are almost impossible to see when they aren't moving. Most arid-zone birds, or birds of the dry west, are also adapted to drink saline water and have mechanisms by which they can excrete high concentrations of salt.

Endangered species

The riverine rabbit (*Bunolagus monticularis*) is endemic to the central Karoo area. This endangered animal's habitat is dominated by river ganna (*Salsola glabrescens*) and kareedoring (*Lycium* spp.) shrubs that grow on alluvial soils adjacent to seasonally dry watercourses. Destruction of these areas by ploughing for cultivation has halved the original distribution range of the riverine rabbit.

Migrations

During the 1700s and even the 1800s, travellers and hunters recorded sightings of migratory springbok (*Antidorcas marsupialis*), throughout most of the Nama karoo. These vast herds – called 'trekbokken' – moved between the summer and winter rainfall regions, but not on a regular, annual basis. It is possible that the springbok were egged on by a combination of high population numbers and periods of drought, when the veld condition in the Nama karoo and southern Kalahari was poor. Sadly, these large-scale migrations are no longer seen as springbok numbers dramatically declined at the turn of the 20th century, when thousands of these animals were hunted because they competed with sheep for grazing. Their movement was further restricted by the fencing of farms in the Nama karoo.

Other migratory species included black wildebeest (*Connochaetes gnou*), and blesbok (*Damaliscus dorcas phillipsi*). The now extinct quagga (*Equus quagga*) too was once found in Bushmanland, where herds of up to 100 were common. (This species had almost reached extinction in the Great Karoo by 1860, and is, of course, extinct today.)

ABOVE, FROM LEFT TO RIGHT In 1937, the Mountain Zebra National Park was proclaimed in an area transitional to the Nama karoo and grassland biomes to save this endemic mammal from extinction; Pyrgomorphid grasshoppers protect themselves by secreting a foul-smelling liquid when disturbed; The beautifully coloured bokmakierie.

ABOVE A leopard tortoise.

Bird life

The Nama karoo shares most of its bird species with the succulent karoo biome, and many of its bird species also occur in the grassland, fynbos and savanna biomes. However, two bird species are endemic to the Karoo, and both are uncommon and could possibly be rare. The cinnamon-breasted warbler (*Euryptila subcinnamomea*) is a cocky, attractive little bird found only on rocky hillsides covered with shrubs, and in dry river gullies and gorges. Sclater's lark (*Spizocorys sclateri*) is a real 'little brown job' found on stony plains and ridges in arid shrublands.

Another bird that is uncommon and highly localised is the red lark (*Certhilauda burra*). It is endemic to the scrub-covered red sand dunes and surrounding karroid shrublands of Bushmanland and northeastern Namaqualand. Ludwig's bustard (*Neotis ludwigii*) migrates seasonally between the Nama karoo (where it nests from about August) and the

ECOLOGICAL THREATS AND DESERTIFICATION

The main ecological threats in the Nama karoo biome are those resulting from agriculture, the spread of invasive alien plants, mining operations in certain areas, succulent plant collecting, and the illegal collection of reptiles for the pet trade, all of which lead to a loss of biotic diversity.

Widespread invasive alien plant species, such as the poisonous wild tobacco (Nicotiana glauca), occur along drainage lines, riverbanks and flood plains, as well as along roadsides and other disturbed areas. These plants invade once the indigenous plant cover has been reduced by poor farming practices. Mesquite (Prosopis glandulosa) is common along the Orange River, Bushmanland, and in the drier areas of the Nama karoo where it has been planted as a source of fodder. Jointed cactus (Opuntia aurantiaca), which is common in the eastern parts of the biome, is spread vegetatively rather than by seed, as the seeds are sterile. The fruits and spiny leaf-pads, which are easily broken off, are able to root and form new plants.

Veld deterioration has resulted in encroachment and bush thickening (or densification) by shrubs such as threethorn shrub (Rhigozum trichotomum), black thorn (Acacia mellifera subsp. detinens) and bitterbos (Chrysocoma ciliata). Densification by driedoring suppresses perennial grass production as a result of competition for soil moisture, which in turn decreases grazing capacity by between 43 and 93 per cent. Black thorn has a similar effect.

The various forms of agriculture probably pose the major ecological threat in the Nama karoo biome. Riparian bush is rapidly being destroyed along the Orange River, and large areas have been transformed by the development of irrigation lands on the flood plains. Water run-off from these cultivated lands results in an accumulation of pesticides and toxic chemicals in the rivers. Fish absorb these chemicals, causing an indirect negative effect on the numbers of their natural predator, the African fish eagle (Haliaeetus vocifer). The spraying of pesticides such as benzine hexachloride (BHC) for the control of brown locusts (Locustana paradalina) has a major impact on the fauna of the biome.

Because the poisons persist for long periods of time, they are concentrated up the food chain, making birds and animals at the top of the chain, such as carnivores, vultures and eagles, most vulnerable to their toxic effects.

Considerable small-stock losses caused by problem animals, such as black-backed jackal (Canis mesomelas) and caracal (Felis caracal), are widespread. The incorrect and indiscriminate use of poisons by farmers in controlling these predators, however, results in mortalities of many nontarget species. Secondary poisoning of eagles and vultures, which feed on the carcasses of target species or the poisoned bait, also occurs.

There is often conflict between small-stock farmers and eagles, particularly when their home ranges extend onto private land where they are sometimes poisoned or shot. Martial eagles (Polemaetus bellicosus) and black or Verreaux's eagles (Aquila verreauxii) occur throughout the Nama karoo and play an important role in controlling prey populations such as dassies and hares, which can overutilise the vegetation and compete with domestic stock for grazing. Grazing pressure by domestic livestock has eliminated or drastically reduced the grass component in parts of the Nama karoo. It is estimated that the grazing capacity of the Karoo has decreased between 30 and 50 per cent as a result of vegetation deterioration. In some areas the grass component does seem to recover if grazing pressures are well managed, however other areas have been transformed from grassland to karroid shrubland, and are unlikely to revert to their former state even in the absence of grazing. The possible spread of karoo shrubland in an easterly direction into the sweet grassveld of the northeastern Cape and southern Free State, and the development of deserts in the western and northwestern parts of the Nama karoo are important topics of discussion lately, within conservation circles.

Selective grazing, overstocking and trampling all cause soil erosion in areas where the vegetation cover has been reduced, the replacement of palatable plant species with less palatable species, and a loss of species diversity.

succulent karoo biomes, where it settles for winter, when the quality of the vegetation is better and insect populations increase.

Other open-country birds typical of the Nama karoo, include species like the Karoo korhaan (*Eupodotis vigorsii*), Burchell's courser (*Cursorius rufus*), blue crane (*Anthropoides paradisea*), thick-billed lark (*Galerida magnirostris*), Karoo lark (*Certhilauda albescens*), grey-backed finch-lark (*Eremopterix verticalis*), black-eared finch-lark (*E. australis*), southern grey tit (*Parus afer*), Karoo chat (*Cercomela schlegelii*), sickle-winged chat (*C. sinuata*), Layard's titbabbler (*Parisoma layardi*), Karoo robin (*Erythropygia coryphaeus*), fairy flycatcher (*Stenostira scita*), Karoo eremomela (*Eremomela gregalis*), rufous-eared warbler (*Malcorus pectoralis*), Namaqua prinia (*Phragmacia substriata*), spotted prinia (*Prinia maculosa*), rock pipit (*Anthus crenatus*), bokmakierie (*Telophorus zeylonus*), pale-winged starling (*Onychognatus nabouroup*), and black-headed canary (*Serinus alario*).

Insects

Insects that have a significant impact on the vegetation of the Nama karoo are the Karoo caterpillar (*Loxostega frustalis*), the brown locust (*Locustana pardalina*), and the harvester termite (*Hodotermes mossambicus*). 'Heuweltjies' are raised mounds that are probably formed by the activities of termites, and their soils are further altered by burrowing animals. The termitaria consist of finer textured, alkaline soils that contain significantly more organic matter and have higher moister contents and water holding capacity than surrounding soils. These changes in soil result in heuweltjies supporting different vegetation.

Interestingly, extensive drought periods followed by good rains encourage the occurance of brown locust irruptions (see box on page 88), while similar situations cause termite populations to crash. Brown locusts produce a total potential seasonal frass (excrement) in the order of 2.2 million tons, which could cover 87 per cent of the Karoo in a season.

Succulent Karoo

Annelise le Roux and Gretel van Rooyen

The succulent karoo has been described as the most species-rich desert-like region on earth.
This biome covers approximately 81 527 square kilometres in the western part of South Africa,
and represents approximately 20 per cent of the flora found in the whole of the southern African region.
Of its about 5 000 species, some 40 per cent are endemic. The geology, topography and rainfall within the
succulent karoo vary greatly, but there are common factors: a low winter rainfall, extreme summer aridity,
and lime-rich, weakly developed soils. Seemingly against all odds, this arid, harsh environment explodes
with colour during one brief, annual season, to become an unparalleled floral spectacle.

GEOGRAPHICAL REGIONS
The succulent karoo biome can be divided into six distinct
geographical regions.

Namaqualand
Namaqualand hugs the northwestern corner of South Africa, and itself
can be divided into four regions, namely Richtersveld, Sandveld, the hills
and mountains of the Kamiesberg range and the Knersvlakte (see box on
page 106). This area is world famous for its spring flower display and
diversity of plant life. About 3 500 plant species are found in Namaqualand,
of which 22 per cent are endemic. Of the five centres of endemism
identified in the succulent karoo biome, three are found here.

Western mountain karoo
This area forms a plateau west of the Bokkeveld Mountains, east of
the Renoster River, south of Bushmanland and north of Sutherland.
The region is characterised by very fertile, red clay soils interspersed
with dolerite outcrops.

Due to its higher elevation, the climate is both cooler and wetter
than that of Namaqualand. It usually receives more than 400 millimetres
of rainfall a year. The vegetation cover is generally dense, and the flora
is dominated by geophytic (bulbous) species such as the red-orange
katstert (*Bulbinella latifolia* var. *doloritica*) of the Nieuwoudtville area.

Of the 163 endemic plant species found in the western mountain
Karoo region, 30 per cent are geophytes.

ABOVE *Sunrise in Namaqualand. This low-rainfall region receives most of its precipitation in winter.*

Roggeveld

This is the most easterly of the winter rainfall areas. The Roggeveld lies at a high altitude, and stretches from Calvinia to Sutherland. The vegetation is an evergreen, non-succulent shrubland. The wild rye or 'wilde rog' (*Secale africana*), after which the area is named, has become scarce and needs special attention to prevent it from becoming extinct. The star tree (*Cliffortia arborea*), an unusual bush with needle-like leaves, is confined to the mountains of this region. A number of endemic plant species have been recorded in this area. On the whole, however, knowledge of the vegetation in the Roggeveld is very limited.

Tanqua karoo

A very arid interior plain, the Tanqua karoo lies in the rain shadow of the Cederberg. It rarely receives more than 50 millimetres of rain a year. Perennial species are few and far between, but occasional winter storms can transform this barren desert into a floral display of annual species.

Little Karoo

The Little Karoo is banded by the Swartberg range to the north and the Langeberg to the south, from Montagu in the west to Uniondale in the east. The western portion of the Little Karoo receives predominantly winter rainfall, whereas the eastern portion receives most of its rainfall in autumn and early summer.

Average rainfall in the Little Karoo is much higher than in the rest of the succulent karoo biome, and more than 400 millimetres a year have been recorded in some places. The effect of this is clearly seen in the dense vegetation in the western portion of this area.

Some parts of the Little Karoo are covered with spekboom (*Portulacaria afra*), and on dry, rocky hillsides, scattered small trees such as guarri (*Euclea undulata*), wild plum (*Pappea capensis*), and weeping boer-bean (*Schotia afra*) are found. The eastern reaches of the Little Karoo is scattered with white quartz pebbles, mimicked by endemic plants such as *Gibbaeum* spp. and *Muiria hortensae*.

The Little Karoo is considered a centre of endemism with 168 plant species found only in this region.

WILD FLOWERS

A barren land for most of the year, the succulent karoo becomes a floral wonderland for a few weeks in early spring.

Namaqualand, especially, has become synonymous with spectacular colour displays of wild flowers. The best displays usually occur from early August to mid-September.

The precursor of a good flower season is good rainfall in autumn (April and May), followed by regular winter rains.

The timing of the first substantial rainfall is highly unpredictable, but the sooner the first rains fall, the earlier the flowering season. Since favourable conditions for seed germination of ephemeral species can occur over a long period, the growth period of these plants can last six to eight months in a year when the rainy season starts in autumn. When the rainy season starts in mid-winter, it may last only two to three months.

Weather patterns determine the duration of the flower season, and accurate predictions on how long a season will last cannot be made. Wind is an important element in Namaqualand and hot berg-wind conditions can cause an abrupt end to the flower season.

The area is unique in that it is the only desert in the world to have such an extravagant and diverse spring flower display. Namaqualand encompasses one of the most interesting plant assemblages in Africa, not least of all because plant species have been forced to adapt to specific habitats or microhabitats, and as a result a large number of endemics exist in this area. In total 118 families occur, of which 58 of the 730 genera and about 2 000 of the species are endemic.

Worcester-Robertson karoo

This region lies in the valleys of the Cape Fold Mountains, which are covered with fynbos vegetation. Shales and quartzites are the dominant geological formations and, together with the higher rainfall, these produce a fairly luxuriant shrubland. Probably due to the surrounding mountain vegetation, the Worcester-Robertson karoo shows far greater affinities with the Cape Flora than any other in the succulent karoo biome.

CONSERVATION

Through knowledge comes understanding, awareness and caring. Not enough is known about the weird and wonderful plants of the succulent karoo. Not only do we not know exactly how they function and survive, we have not even discovered and described all the species. Research and knowledge is essential for the survival of these odd plants. The challenge of cultivating these plants (not eradicating them from the veld) to further enrich our surroundings, is enormous.

Because each area within the succulent karoo biome features unique scenery and plant species composition, it is essential that a network of reserves protect this heritage.

A number of protected areas already exist. They vary in conservation status but all contribute to the preservation of species, and provide opportunities for ecotourism, recreation and education.

Different vegetation types and habitats of Namaqualand are represented in present conservation areas, such as the Richtersveld National Park, the Goegap Provincial Nature Reserve and the Namaqua National Park. It is intended to add a Groen River National Park and a provincial nature reserve in the Knersvlakte to the Namaqualand conservation areas.

The Hantam Mountain and its endemics are protected in the Akkerendam Local Nature Reserve at Calvinia, in the western mountain karoo region.

Although the Tanqua karoo has a national park, much of the vegetation within this region is not yet conserved.

The Worcester-Robertson karoo is represented by the Vrolijkheid Provincial Nature Reserve.

The Anysberg and Gamkapoort provincial nature reserves, both representing major portions of this region, are found in the Little Karoo.

This arid area, with its interesting and challenging adaptations to ensure survival, can be an enormous nature school, tailor-made for ecotourism. However, without understanding and care for this unpolished jewel, a renewable resource will be destroyed.

The Aizoaceae is by far the largest plant family in the succulent karoo (also the largest in southern Africa). It includes the vygie, or former Mesembryanthemaceae family. This family of low-growing perennials with succulent leaves and stems, includes 102 genera and 861 species. The second largest family is the daisy family, or Asteraceae. It has 90 genera and 648 species.

The two largest genera in the succulent karoo biome are *Ruschia* (136 species) and *Conophytum* (116 species), both of the vygie family. The well-known genus *Oxalis* (sorrels or 'surings'), has 114 geophytic species while *Crassula* has 110 species.

OPPOSITE Near Springbok, pietsnot flowers form a tiny yellow island in a sea of orange Namaqualand daisies. Pietsnot has a slimy root which is much sought after by duikers.

ABOVE The rich light of the dying sun lingers on the rock wall of a remote kloof (cleft or steep-sided valley) in the Richtersveld.

UNIQUE LIFE STRATEGIES AND ADAPTATIONS

Rainfall within the biome varies from 50 to 350 millimetres annually. Most of this rain falls during the months from May to August. Temperature extremes vary from minus 5°C to over 40°C. Fog, which is frequent along the coast, is an important source of moisture where the annual rainfall is less than 100 millimetres.

The low rainfall, together with extreme summer aridity, are two of the main factors that influence life forms in the succulent karoo biome. Accordingly, the plants and animals that live here have adapted to their harsh environment. These adaptations have resulted in a worldwide interest in this unique area. The two main survival strategies of plants growing in harsh arid conditions are: evasion through ephemerality, versus tolerance through succulence. Drought evasion or avoidance is commonly found among the annual species, while succulence is exhibited by perennial species.

Evasion

In contrast to the perennial flora in arid regions, annuals are often considered to exhibit no striking adaptations to their arid climate. Instead, they are seen to escape unfavourable conditions by rapid

ABOVE Shiny rock plates create an austere scene in the Richtersveld. The region has an extremely complex geology.

ABOVE One of the most extraordinary succulents of the Richtersveld, the halfmens can grow up to two metres tall and reach an age of 150 years or older.

completion of their life cycles during the brief periods when conditions are favourable for growth.

Annuals, therefore, synchronise their life cycle with that of the climate. They germinate, grow, flower and set seed during the moist winter and spring, then die off, surviving the dry period in the form of seed. To ensure their survival in an environment where the rainfall

is unpredictable – in timing, amount and space – the annual species of Namaqualand have evolved certain characteristics to combat the year-to-year variability in habitat conditions.

A high percentage of the seeds of most annual Namaqualand species of are dormant, and this prevents all the seed from germinating simultaneously after one good shower It is further believed that the

ABOVE In the Biedouw Valley, an arid hill is transformed by a golden carpet of teebossie.

seeds of many annual species are long-lived and are able to remain in the soil without loss of viability for many years. Many other species also have germination regulating mechanisms, which ensure that germination only occurs under specific environmental conditions. And, because each species has its own specific temperature at which germination takes place, different species are favoured in different years, depending on the timing of the first rains. It is believed that the floristic composition of the annual vegetation in Namaqualand in a particular year is determined by the interaction between the timing and intensity of rainfall on the one hand, and the temperature at the time of the rainfall on the other. The effect of the precipitation depends not only on the amount of rainfall but also on its duration. A slow rain is more effective in bringing germination about than is a cloudburst yielding the same precipitation total.

A number of species are found among the annuals of Namaqualand that produce morphologically differing types of seeds. Perhaps the best-known example occurs within the genus *Dimorphotheca*, commonly known as the Namaqualand daisy. Here the flowers on the margin of the flower head produce one type of seed, and the flowers in the centre of the flower head (central part of the flower head) another. These seeds differ not only with regard to dispersal but also in germination behaviour. Even the plants grown from the different types of seeds have different traits. Seeds from the central flowers are winged and can be dispersed over large distances. They germinate easily and produce competitively superior plants. Seeds from the marginal flowers are unwinged and are not widely dispersed, nor do they germinate easily, and the seeds produce competitively inferior plants.

ABOVE Travelling northwards towards the Orange River, the visitor to the Richtersveld is confronted by this forbidding landscape, with its mocking mirages.

Tolerance

Succulent plants are more drought tolerant than annuals, for during drought periods they are able to live off the water stored in their leaves or stems.

To help retain the moisture in succulents, different strategies have evolved. Most species have a thick outer skin or cuticle, either waxy or hairy, with few stomata to prevent water loss. Some, on the other hand, have adopted a photosynthetic pathway differing from that of most other plants, and only take in carbon dioxide at night when it is cooler, thus preventing water loss through their open stomata.

One of the dominant and endemic succulent families in the succulent karoo, the vygies, exhibits many adaptations to prevent water loss. Some

ABOVE The Richtersveld's many geological formations are of both volcanic and sedimentary origin, and consist mainly of granites, gneisses, limestones, schists, layered shales and scatterings of white quartz.

of the species do not have a thick skin but have many large cells filled with water, called bladder cells. While moisture is not limiting, these cells are thick and swollen, standing almost upright. The stomata, which are used for carbon dioxide intake and transpiration, lie between these cells. When drought sets in, these cells 'wilt', falling flat and covering the stomata – thus preventing water loss.

Other vygies, called stone plants, are very small, have one or two leaves per plant and never grow much higher than soil level. They are very proficient at recycling their water: when drought sets in, the water from the exposed leaves is withdrawn into the following year's leaves, which are protected in the middle of the plant and lie underground. The old dried-out leaves become pale and papery, serving to protect the following year's leaves during summer. The whitish colour of this layer also acts as a sun reflector.

Windowplants, found along the coast of Namaqualand, take evasion one step further. In summer they withdraw underground totally, and even in winter when it is wetter, they will not grow above the level of the soil. All that is exposed to the air is a small, round transparent 'window' that lets the sunlight in. The sunlight is used in the process of photosynthesis by the underground side walls of the leaves that contain chlorophyll pigments.

Another striking feature of vygies is their highly specialised dispersal mechanism, that is linked to rainfall. In an arid environment such a mechanism should have an advantage because dispersal can then only occur when water is available and conditions for germination are, theoretically, favourable.

Most vygies produce seeds that are enclosed in 'capsules' that open when the weather becomes moist and close as soon as it dries out. The opening action of the capsules is controlled by a special tissue, which absorbs moisture and causes the valves to move outwards. The seeds are dispersed by raindrops as they fall onto these opened capsules.

In the primitive capsule types the seeds lie exposed in the open locules and are ejected by a splash-cup action. A few well-landed raindrops can empty this type of capsule very quickly. In the more sophisticated capsule types, the seeds in the open capsule do not lie fully exposed but are covered by an elastic membrane at the top of the locule. When a raindrop falls onto the covering membrane the seeds in these capsules are ejected over a far greater distance by a springboard action. However, this mechanism allows only a few seeds to be dispersed at a time and a large proportion of the seeds are retained in the capsule after a rain storm – an adaptation that simultaneously encourages dispersal in space, but inhibits dispersal in time.

Non-succulent dwarf shrubs have also developed adaptations to survive the drought. These shrubs either have small leaves, which limit the area from which transpiration can occur, or large leaves, which they shed during the dry summer months. Some plants have virtually no leaves but rather have green stems in which photosynthesis occurs and transpiration is minimal. Geophytes survive the summer underground in the form of bulbs, corms, rhizomes or tubers. They can therefore be classified as both evasive and tolerant organisms.

BELOW The chat flycatcher is one of the most characteristic birds of the arid, western parts of South Africa.

BOTTOM Conophytum flavum subsp. flavum specialises in colonising rock crevices.

THREATS

*B*ecause many of the plant species found in the succulent karoo biome are specialised, any change in their surroundings will affect them, usually adversely.

Larger bushes protect and act as 'nurse plants' for the germination and survival of the seedlings of some shrub species. Grazing reduces the vegetation cover, robbing plants of protection and shade, and undoubtedly will result in the disappearance of some plant species. Indiscriminate grazing at the wrong time of the year can cause the disappearance of an entire seedling crop, because seedlings are the most sought-after fodder in a desert environment. While the stone plants are not edible, trampling can easily eradicate them.

Humans, too, pose an enormous threat to the unique succulent plants of this biome, particularly in the form of collectors. Most small succulent plants reach ages of up to 50 years, and recruitment may take place only once or twice in their lifetime. To add to this, these plants are usually restricted to small areas, and it is possible for a collector to remove an entire population of a species in a single field excursion. These plants will, in any event, not survive outside of their biome, and if removed from the veld, could lead to extinction of the species.

Although there are only a few alien plants in the succulent karoo, their presence is a real and major threat. Wild tobacco (Nicotiana glauca) and oleander (Nerium oleander) can be seen along dry river and stream beds. Other invasive species such as blue thistle (Argemone ochroleuca) and fumatory, or duiwelkerwel (Fumaria muralis) are found in disturbed areas, usually abandoned fields.

An abundance of kraalbos (Galenia africana), asbos (Psilocaulon spp.), soutslaai (Mesembryanthemum guerichianum) and/or swartstamvy (Ruschia robusta), which are all indigenous species, indicates overutilisation of the vegetation. In order to encourage recovery of the natural diversity of the vegetation in the areas dominated by any of these species, grazing should be curtailed to a minimum.

ABOVE Throughout the Richtersveld the vegetation is, on average, less than 50 centimetres high and characterised by a large variety of succulents. With at least 363 species found only in the Richtersveld, this region is considered an important centre of endemism.

WILDLIFE

If the annuals of the succulent karoo biome have successfully evolved various adaptations to optimise their chances of survival, so too have some animals. The two species of rain frog that occur along the West Coast have developed an evasive survival strategy, in which they live under the moist dune sand, only surfacing to feed at night when there is heavy fog, thereby ensuring that their skin stays moist.

The animal life in this biome is not nearly as rich as the plant life, and, although the succulent karoo possesses a very rich insect life, very little is known about this group.

However, 65 species of mammals (three endemic), 252 species of birds, 12 of amphibians (one endemic) and 108 of reptiles (eight endemic), have been recorded for the succulent karoo biome.

Namaqualand has a reputation for being one of the richest areas for reptile species in southern Africa.

The presence of regularly spaced circular patches, or mima mounds that measure 10 to 15 metres in diameter, are a prominent feature of the succulent karoo. Much is speculated about the origin of these 'heuweltjies', but the most acceptable argument seems to be that they are mounds made by termites. The presence of termites can alter the soil composition, with calcrete forming in these mounds, making tunneling easier here than in the surrounding loose sand.

The succulent karoo biome does not have a unique avifauna – it shares most of its bird species with the Nama karoo biome, and some with the fynbos biome. However, many species endemic to southern Africa occur in the succulent karoo.

REGIONS OF NAMAQUALAND

Richtersveld

The Richtersveld is tucked away in the very northwestern corner of South Africa and Namaqualand, bound in the north by the Orange River and by the Atlantic Ocean to the west. Port Nolloth, Steinkopf and Vioolsdrif are situated on the southern and eastern limits.

This region is very mountainous, and its many geological formations are of both volcanic and sedimentary origin, and consist mainly of granites, gneisses, limestones, schists, layered shales and scatterings of white quartz. Through the

centuries erosion has created a harsh, rugged, yet colourful and beautiful scenery. It is a low rainfall area, averaging less than 50 millimetres a year, although a good shower can result in the appearance of a carpet of flowers. Throughout the area the vegetation is, on average, less than 50 centimetres high, and is known for the large variety of succulents, not only in terms of species but also in terms of growth form. These succulents are mainly the vygies, stonecrops (crassulas) and pelargoniums. With at least 363 species found only in the Richtersveld, this region – known as the Gariep Centre – is considered an important centre of endemism.

Sandveld

The Sandveld forms a coastal strip of about 30 kilometres in width along the Atlantic Ocean, from the Orange River in the north to south of Elands Bay. The substrate is loose, white sand at the coast changing to red sand inland. The interior comprises a loamy, calcareous, rich soil in a slightly undulating landscape.

Rain falls during the winter months and increases as it moves southwards, varying from less than 50 millimetres between the Orange River and Port Nolloth, to between 50 and 100 millimetres a year southwards to the Groen River, and between 100 and 150 millimetres near the Olifants River. South of here it increases to 300 millimetres a year.

The meagre coastal rainfall is supplemented by fog, which is generated by the cold Benguela Current that sweeps up the coastline from the south. Right at the coast the vegetation is usually low, only about 30 centimetres high, and sjielingbos (Zygophyllum cordifolium), several species of Drosanthemum, melkbos (Euphorbia karroensis), and karoorapuis (Othonna sedifolia) are generally found here. Further inland the vegetation is, on average, one-metre high, and t'arra-t'kooi (Stoeberia frutescens) is the most common vygie bush.

Other species also found in this area are the skilpadbos (Zygophyllum morgsana), ossierapuis (Othonna cylindrica) and other shrubby vygies, in particular, Lampranthus suavissimus and volstruisvygie (Cephalophyllum spongiosum), are common.

Kamiesberg

The Kamiesberg range consists of distinctive round, rocky, granite hills separated by sandy plains. Many of these rocky hills have conspicuous large, flat, or sometimes rounded, rock surfaces. This region can be regarded as an escarpment about 50 kilometres wide, which separates the low-lying Sandveld from the Bushmanland plateau. It stretches from south of Steinkopf to just south of Bitterfontein. Rainfall varies from 100 to 200 millimetres a year, although some of the high-lying areas can receive up to 400 millimetres.

Vegetation reaches heights of between 0.5 and one metre, and is slightly higher in the rocky hills than on the plains. The most common dwarf shrub found on the plains is kraalbos (Galenia africana). It is considered a pioneer plant, as it is the first perennial to colonise abandoned fields. Because small stock does not utilise kraalbos it is also the only perennial remaining on very badly overgrazed, disturbed or degraded areas.

STRANGE PLANTS OF THE RICHTERSVELD

The halfmens (Pachypodium namaquanum) is the probably the best-known succulent of the Richtersveld. This spiny, usually single-stemmed succulent can grow up to two metres tall, and can live for as long as 150 years. Its leaves, clumped together at the top of the plant, always point to the north in order to utilize the sun to its maximum. Seen from a distance this 'head' of leaves appears human – giving rise to the tree's common name, 'halfmens', or 'half-human'.

The survival of this curious plant hangs in the balance because of unscrupulous collection without consideration for age or the fact that the tree does not transplant well. Although the seeds of the halfmens germinate well, the survival rate of seedlings in the veld is low. One of the reasons for this is that, although the halfmens is easily cultivated, man is impatient and would rather collect a grown tree than wait for the seedlings to grow into a full-sized tree.

Another rare and threatened plant of this area of the succulent karoo biome is the bastard quiver tree (Aloe pillansii). This species is the tallest of the quiver trees – it sometimes reaches heights of up to 10 metres, with a single stem and a cluster of branches laden with leaves at the top – and it is restricted to a small section of the Richtersveld. The population is very static and new plants seldom manage to establish themselves.

The bastard quiver tree and its close relatives, the quiver tree, also known as the kokerboom (A. dichotoma), and the maiden's quiver tree (A. ramosissima) are three succulent species that belong to the monocotyledons (monocots), a group of plants that include the grasses, lilies, palms and orchids. Unlike other plants, monocotyledonous trees are unable to develop a compact woody stem. Instead these stems are very fibrous. Quiver trees have many traditonal uses: the hollowed out branches made natural quivers for Bushman (San) hunter's arrows (hence the name); the fibrous water-absorbent material of the trunk is a natural insulator and is used to line the walls of coolboxes, and in the absence of wood for building, as walls for housing. Examples of these houses can still be found in the Rooifontein area of the Kamiesberg.

ABOVE *The grandeur of the Richtersveld: an arid hillside, strewn with crumbling quartz and graced by immense specimens of the rare bastard quiver tree, is thrown in sharp relief against a pastel-hued backdrop of distant mountains.*

Other dominant species, especially in the hills, are kapokbos (Eriocephalus ericoides), skaapbos (Tripteris sinuatum *and* T. oppositifolium), perdebos (Didelta spinosa), skilpadbos, fluitjiesbos (Lebeckia sericea) as well as many vygies of the Aizoaceae family, such as Ruschia, Leipoldtia and Drosanthemum species. A few of the conspicuous and abundant ephemerals are pietsnot (Grielum humifusum), dassiegousblomme (Tripteris amplectens *and* T. hyoseroides), Namaqualand daisy (Dimorphotheca sinuata), hongerblom (Senecio arenarius), teebossie (Leysera tenella) and many sporrie species (Heliophila spp.).

The Kamiesberg range is home to 201 endemic species, and the central mountain is an endemic centre with 79 species confined to this small area.

Knersvlakte

The Knersvlakte lies between Vanrhynsdorp and Nuwerus and, from west to east, between the Sandveld and the Bokkeveld Mountains near Nieuwoudtville. It covers approximately 4 500 square kilometres.

The landscape is typified by very low, rolling hills covered with small, white quartz pebbles and very saline soils.

The meagre rainfall varies from 100 to 200 millimetres a year.

The vegetation is extremely low (from 10 to 50 centimetres high), yet the area sustains a phenomenal variety of succulents that are adapted to survive the intense heat of summer and the saline soils.

In the quartz patches there are 'unplantlike' succulents such as bokkloutjies (Argyroderma spp.), krapogies (Oophytum oviforme) and baboon-fingers (Dactylopsis digitata).

Many other vygies are found in the Knersvlakte, along with the odd daisy (Asteraceae) shrub. Each quartz patch may have its own species composition and even the size of the white quartz pebbles determines which species are present. There are 140 endemic species in the Knersvlakte, of which four per cent have only been discovered in the last five years. This centre of endemism is known as the Vanrhynsdorp Endemic Centre.

Thicket

Roy A Lubke

Tall euphorbias resembling giant candelabra entirely surrounded by an almost impenetrable growth of lowish bush, are the main characteristics of the thicket biome. This vegetation covers approximately 41 888 square kilomeres, or a mere 0.03 per cent, of the southern African region. Thicket does not form a continuous zone, and extends in a somewhat fragmented band along the eastern and southern coast from KwaZulu-Natal down into the Western Cape, with fingers extending into the Nama karoo. It is most extensive, though, in the Eastern Cape, particularly around the famous Addo Elephant National Park and other conserved areas.

Thicket is not recognised in scientific literature as a biome in its own right, but there are areas in South Africa where the term conveniently describes a characteristic vegetation type that, although exhibiting close affinities with adjacent biomes such as forest, savanna, karoo and fynbos, is significantly different from them.

For example, thicket cannot be described as forest as the rainfall is too low and the vegetation does not have the required height or the many strata below the canopy. Forests tend to be more open with distinct layers of trees and shrubs, whereas thicket is denser and occurs where rainfall is lower, usually at lower altitudes of mountains and in river valleys.

Neither can thicket be described as savanna since there is no distinct grassy ground layer that is so typical of this vegetation type. Although

grasses may sometimes be present in thicket, these only tend to occur as scattered individuals. Many of the woody thicket species are invasive, however, and where thicket abuts savanna and grassland areas, there is a transitional zone between thicket and these neighbouring vegetation types.

Thicket also often forms a mosaic with fynbos, especially in coastal areas, where it occurs on the deeper sands or moist soil types, which can support the woody tree and shrub species. Subtropical thicket is, therefore, a transition vegetation, best described as a closed shrubland to low forest in which evergreen succulent trees are dominant.

Also a feature of thicket vegetation are shrubs and vines, many of which have stem spines. Density is also a major characteristic of thicket and the invariably multistemmed trees and shrubs, three to seven metres

ABOVE Crassula arborescens.

ABOVE *Bright red inflorescences of* Schotia afra.

tall, are often so closely interlaced that they form an all but impenetrable plant community, except along tracks made by animals.

The overall controlling factor producing thicket rather than forest or savanna is rainfall. In the Eastern Cape, thicket occurs in the drier regions where rainfall is too erratic or too low for the development of forest. It is particularly abundant in the river valleys where there is protection from fires and there is sufficient soil to support woody vegetation. Often much of the moisture obtained during the dry periods comes from valley mists and fogs that frequent these valleys.

Thicket, therefore, is a product of presently prevailing climatic conditions. In temperate or subtropical conditions if rainfall was to increase or become more regular, the trees would flourish and distinct strata or layers would form in the thicket, changing it to forest. A regular seasonal rainfall with a dry, cold winter, on the other hand, would favour the formation of savanna.

The thicket most commonly encountered is that along the coastal dunes. If you have ever tried to make or find a path from a car park down to the dunes or sea, you will appreciate what thicket is like. The short, low shrubs, often evergreen and sometimes succulent, are dense and intertwined. Often they are armed with stem spines. Vines with sharp thorns tear skin and clothing, while here and there the bright flowers of some bushes lend colour to the dense, impenetrable mass of greenery.

In the inland valleys, hardy goats and cattle manage to penetrate the thicket, and exploring the terrain in these regions requires creeping low along their paths to get under the sharp thorny and succulent shrubs. The lower-growing thicket of the inland valleys may form circular clumps of bush, but on the moist slopes they coalesce, forming an impenetrable mass. Very often a great diversity of species is made up of many succulents and dwarf Karoo-like plants.

TYPES OF THICKET
Five different types of subtropical thicket are described.

Dune Thicket
Dune thicket is probably the most widespread, but it occupies a very small area because it is confined to the narrow, seaward facing side of coastal dunes. Species growing here are able to withstand high winds and salt spray. Under high salt conditions, many of the woody tree species develop succulent leaves. In protected areas and under higher rainfall conditions this type of thicket is replaced by coastal forest.

The important species in the dune thicket are the coastal white milk-wood (*Sideroxylon inerme*) and, extending down the KwaZulu-Natal coast as far as Port Alfred, the coastal red milkwood (*Mimusops caffra*). Also following this distribution pattern is the coast silver oak (*Brachylaena discolor*) and KwaZulu-Natal wild banana (*Strelitzia nicolai*).

South Africa's coastline is prime land for urban development and tourism, and dune thicket is often transformed into suburbs, holiday resorts and caravan parks. As a consequence little thicket is conserved, except within coastal reserves. Owners of cottages along the coast would be well advised to disturb as little of the coastal thicket as possible. Not only would they be making a significant contribution to conservation, but they would also benefit by encouraging a hardy vegetation type, requiring little care and gardening effort. Moreover, the abundance of birds and small animals would still have a home and holiday makers would be able to enjoy watching wildlife on their trips to the coast.

Valley thicket
Valley thicket extends from the coast up the river valleys and generally has a higher canopy of trees. The large succulent tree euphorbias

ABOVE A milk bush creeper.

ABOVE The pretty flowers of the spekboom.

(*Euphorbia triangularis* and *E. tetragona*) are common in this vegetation type, along with many other woody trees and shrubs.

A number of cultivated indigenous hedges, such as *Plumbago auriculata* and Cape honeysuckle (*Tecomaria capensis*) have their origins in this thicket type.

Valley thicket is often cleared for agriculture purposes, but there is still a large proportion preserved in reserves, both in KwaZulu-Natal and in the Eastern Cape. Its greatest threat is in the Eastern Cape where trees are removed by local communities for building houses or for firewood. Often only the soft succulent euphorbia species remain standing.

Xeric succulent thicket
The dry succulent thicket or xeric succulent thicket is confined to two areas: the valleys of the Fish and the Sundays rivers, where the dominant plant species are the succulent spekboom (*Portulacaria afra*) and shrub euphorbias. This thicket type contains a high proportion of succulents and is the one most closely related to the karoo biome types.

Mesic succulent thicket
Mesic succulent thicket occurs along the coast, especially around the Sundays River and in the Gamtoos Valley. It is under threat from development as areas have been cleared for coastal resorts.

Spekboom succulent thicket
In the interiors of the Eastern Cape and parts of the Western Cape, spekboom succulent thicket is commonly found on the mountain slopes. Often this is seen as a light green band above the denser dark green shrubs of the valley thicket. Spekboom thrives under these conditions and is the dominant species.

Affinities with other floristic types
Thicket is generally known as subtropical thicket, as it is essentially a subtropical vegetation type that extends down the eastern seaboard of Africa. Although endemism is not a feature of this vegetation type, it is nevertheless of great floristic interest. For example, the plant species of southern African thicket have related species which occur as far away as the Horn of Africa, or the Sahel Region, stretching in a band south of the Sahara Desert.

PLANTS OF THE THICKET

Spekboom (Portulacaria afra) is a common constitute of thicket in inland areas. These branched, soft, woody shrubs have roundish succulent leaves that, it is said, are eaten by African women when they have insufficient natural milk for their babies. Leaves are also dried, ground and used as snuff. Spekboom is valuable fodder for domestic animals, and is a favourite plant of elephant (Loxodonta africana), and many antelope.

Many euphorbia species are found in thicket, including the large candelabra trees. While these are more difficult to cultivate than spekboom, they can make a very attractive feature in a rockery.

Euphorbias have a soft wood and branching, leafless succulent stems, and produce a milky juice. The smaller shrubby forms are browsed on by goats. The milky latex from some species has been used for caulking boats in Mozambique, but the milk is toxic and especially dangerous if it gets in the eye. Some species are dried, ground and used by Xhosa people for various ailments. Two shrubby or scrambling species, Cape honeysuckle (Tecomaria capenses) and the blue flowered Plumbago auriculata are commonly seen in the thicket and are both cultivated as ornamental hedges and shrubs in gardens.

ABOVE   A male malachite sunbird rests on an Aloe africana *flower head.*

ABOVE   The magnificent crane flower, indigenous to the Eastern Cape.

The many karoo plants present in thicket previously saw it classified as a karoo-type vegetation. Thicket species have stronger affinities, though, with the flora of the eastern coastal areas extending from Pondoland to Tongaland and the Cape. These woody shrubs and small trees may even occur in the southern Cape forests and thicket types. Many of the thicket species are only found in KwaZulu-Natal or as far as East London in the Eastern Cape. The greatest diversity of unique species in the thicket, however, is in the Eastern Cape.

ADDO ELEPHANT NATIONAL PARK

*When Addo was proclaimed in 1931, the elephant (*Loxodonta africana*) population stood at 11; today, the park has in excess of 270. Addo has grown over the past decade from 7 700 hectares to more than 50 000 hectares. The largest boost was the inclusion of the former Zuurberg Forest Reserve into the park. Plans are now afoot to increase the conservation area extensively. The objective is to create a greatly enlarged national park that will stretch from the sand dunes at the Sundays River estuary to the succulent Noorsveld and arid Karoo near the Darlington Dam; it will include oceanic regions and the islands in Algoa Bay. This will create an area of immense biological importance, spanning seven biomes, and conserving many of the different forms of coastal and inland thicket and their associated animals, resulting in enormous potential for the development of tourism in the Eastern Cape.*

ANTHONY HALL-MARTIN (AFRICA – ENVIRONMENT & WILDLIFE, VOL.6 NO.6)

WILDLIFE

In bygone times, thicket would have supported many of the large browsers such as black rhinoceros (*Diceros bicornis*), elephant (*Loxodonta africana*) and kudu (*Tragelaphus strepsiceros*). An abundance of these animals kept the woody shrubs and trees in check, especially in the savanna and grassland where thicket is very often invasive today. With the exception of their continued existence in the Addo Elephant National Park, and recent re-introduction at Shamwari Private Game Reserve, these animals have been hunted to extinction in this biome (see 'threats and conservation' box on page 113).

An abundance of bird species and arboreal mammals such as monkeys, galagos, squirrels, and hyrax, are common in thicket. These animals live off the fruits of the trees and play a significant role in seed dispersal, either by dropping the seeds as they feed or in their faeces. For example, woody thicket species generally occur in clumps centred around a bird's perch site such as an ant hill or thorn tree. The birds drop the seeds, and shrubs and bushes grow up around the perch site. As more and more species invade, so the thicket bush clumps coalesce to form dense, impenetrable subtropical thicket.

Although birders will find that watching birds, such as the shrikes, flycatchers and sunbirds is easy in this low, woody vegetation type, it is very difficult to find large mammals in reserves where dense thicket is the dominant vegetation type. Even the elephants of Addo, despite numbering more than 200, are often difficult to observe when they retreat into the dense vegetation.

THREATS AND CONSERVATION

*M*uch concern has been expressed about the conservation of the thicket in the Eastern Cape. In many areas, thicket is under great threat – extensive cattle and goat farming activities, as well as an extensive network of coastal towns and holiday hamlets have destroyed much of this vegetation type.

In the former Transkei area, the greatest threat to the thicket regions is the removal of these thicket patches for firewood, and as this often occurs on steep slopes, it can cause erosion of the river valleys. On the other hand, thicket has spread into areas that used to harbour other vegetation types. If one compares old paintings of the Eastern Cape region with the present distribution of the vegetation types, one will see that the thicket has invaded extensively from the river valleys into the open grasslands.

This is undoubtedly because of the demise of the large browsers such as black rhinoceros (Diceros bicornis) and kudu (Tragelaphus strepsiceros), which would have kept the shrubby plants in check.

The introduction of cattle and sheep meant that only the grasses were being grazed, so the young shrubs were able to thrive. A Grahamstown farmer whose farmstead down in the valley looks out across the hillside speaks of the days when his grandfather could count his cattle on those slopes. Today they would be all hidden, if, in fact, they could find grazing amongst the dense, woody thicket vegetation.

Because of the conservation importance placed on large animals, large areas of thicket – such as the Andries Vosloo Kudu, Sam Knott and Alex Sebe reserves on either side of the Great Fish River in the Eastern Cape are now conserved.

Now combined, these reserves form one of the largest conservation areas in South Africa. The combined reserve is largely undeveloped and provides a haven for many of the different thicket types and conservation of endemic and rare plant species.

Animals such as rhinoceros, kudu and even hippopotamus (Hippopotamus amphibius) have been reintroduced and are preserved in this reserve complex. Even the rare the African rock python (Python sebae) has been relocated here.

Unfortunately, the warthog (Phacochoerus aethiopicus), too has been reintroduced to the Andries Vosloo Kudu Reserve. The warthog, which is thought not to be indigenous to this area, has, due to the lack of natural predators, become abundant, and has to be culled in order to control its burgeoning numbers.

The Addo Elephant National Park (see box on page 112), now linked to the Zuurberg Mountain National Park, is also an extensive area of reserved thicket. Here the thicket grades from the valleys to patches of forest on the protected mountain slopes. In the dry Addo Valley, the original reserve was fenced off in the 1930s using elephant-proof fencing to confine the Addo elephants, because they were raiding neighbouring orange orchards.

ABOVE A view of the Addo bush in the Addo Elephant National Park reveals the typical structure of subtropical thicket.

ABOVE An elephant calf feels with its trunk for the reassuring presence of its mother. The Addo Elephant National Park protects an isolated population of elephants.
BELOW Large succulent tree euphorbias are common in valley thicket.

Evergreen Forests

Coert J Geldenhuys

Lush green foliage, tall trees, monkey ropes, ferns, beautiful but shy birds, a moist, cool and shady environment – this is what comes to mind when someone talks about forests. But what is behind that beauty? Why do these forests form the smallest and most fragmented biome in South Africa? Why are they confined to about 3 000 square kilometres in a narrow strip along the eastern Escarpment and coast from the Soutpansberg and Tongaland in the north to the Cape Peninsula in the south? How do they manage to persist under the pressures of people and the environment?

In South Africa the mixed, evergreen forest system ranges from high forest of over 30 metres to scrub forest with a height of just three metres. This forest system has several very specific characteristics: a mild disturbance regime; a buffered internal microclimate; a shallow root system and closed nutrient cycle; and diverse growth forms organised in layered communities.

FOREST REGIONS

Two main forest regions have been recognised for South Africa. The floras of both regions have strong affinities with the mountain and lowland forests of tropical Africa. Afro-montane forests occur along the Drakensberg Escarpment, the KwaZulu-Natal and Eastern Cape midlands, and southern and southwestern Cape mountains and coastal plateau. Coastal and sand forests occur along the Indian Ocean coastal dunes and lowlands as far south as Port Elizabeth.

Within these broad forest regions, the sizes and species composition of the individual forest patches vary.

FOREST EXTENT

Vegetation maps show the pattern of forest distribution in South Africa to be a large number of small to very small patches, and a few, widely separated, large complexes. The largest forest complex in southern Africa occurs in the southern Cape, between Humansdorp and Mossel Bay, where more than 900 forest patches cover a total area of 60 000 hectares.

ABOVE The Outeniqua yellowwood is the largest of South Africa's forest trees.

The Goudveld-Diepwalle-Harkerville forest to the north and east of Knysna is the largest single continuous forest, comprising 25 700 hectares. Other large forest complexes are the Alexandria forest on coastal dunes east of Port Elizabeth, the Amatole forests of the Eastern Cape mountains, and Grootbosch on the Northern Province Escarpment.

The large forest complexes are separated by narrow to broad zones with no forest or only small, fragmented and isolated forest patches.

Without a doubt, drought, frost and land-use practices that are not reconcilable with forest persistence have, over time, posed barriers to the gene flow amongst the larger, more viable forests.

HISTORICAL DISTRIBUTION

It is commonly believed that the destructive activities of man during the past 100 to 300 years has caused the fragmentation of the forests within the grassland and fynbos biomes. However, the changes in forest area since 1652 (when European traders first set up a permanent station at the Cape) due to human impact are small when compared to changes induced by natural environmental change over millions of years.

One theory is that about 75 million years ago, subtropical and temperate forest covered most of Africa south of the equator. Fossilised pollen, leaves and fruit of forest trees and bones of forest animals found today in various non-forest sites in the region support this. Over this period climate fluctuated between warm and moist periods, when forests expanded, and cold, dry periods when forests retreated. The fragmentation of the forest belt was associated with spread of the savanna, grassland, karoo and fynbos biomes. The forests were most severely limited during the last cold, dry Glacial Period some 18 000 years ago.

FOREST DISTURBANCES – WIND AND FIRE

Forest patches require a minimum of 500 millimetres of rain a year in winter and all-year rainfall areas, and a minimum of 725 millimetres of rain in summer rainfall areas to persist, almost irrespective of the underlying geology. However, the difference between the potential area in which forest could grow and the much smaller actual forest area indicates the impact of disturbances caused by natural and human factors.

A major factor is fire, which is associated with prevailing winds during dry periods. In the southern Cape good examples exist showing that the forests persist in 'shadow' areas of fires associated with berg winds. The greatest berg-wind fire on record in the southern Cape occurred in February 1869, and burnt along the coastal areas from Swellendam to Uitenhage, a distance of about 550 kilometres. While the fire destroyed some forest, much of it escaped unscathed.

Berg winds are gusty, hot, desiccating, generally northwesterly winds that blow from the arid interior across the coastal mountains onto the coast. The mountains alter the flow of the berg winds, channelling them – with greater velocity – southwards through the valleys. South of the mountains, the winds continue in their original flow direction across the coastal platform. Even without fire the berg winds would cause physiological drought for the forest in exposed sites.

When the winds are associated with fire, whether caused by lightning or human action, the fire follows the flow direction of the wind and would destroy forest along that route. Therefore, forests are only able to persist in the 'shadow' areas on the leeward side of the mountains.

A good example is found en route from Plettenberg Bay to Humansdorp. The road leads through luxuriant, dense forest up to the edge of the Storms River. Across the bridge, east of the river, the coastal platform and the slopes of the mountain are devoid of forest, and are covered in the fire-adapted fynbos shrubland.

Sharp breaks of slope also contribute to the persistence of forest on the leeward side to just below the crest, whereas on the leeward side of rounded hills the fire will destroy forest down to the valley bottom. Also, fires would usually follow a course up or down the crest of a ridge, and will not easily burn down or up a narrow valley. An example of such a pattern of burning is found in the mountains behind the Storms River bridge in the Tsitsikamma area. This pattern is typical of forest distribution in this area, but it is also evident throughout southern Africa.

OTHER FOREST DISTURBANCES

The forest interior is subject to regular, small-scale disturbances causing gaps about 50 square metres to 0.5 hectares. Lightning may cause a fire or merely kill a small group of trees. It is interesting that some trees, such as black stinkwood (*Ocotea bullata*), can recover from such strikes by resprouting, whereas others, such as Cape beech (*Rapanea melanophloeos*) are easily killed.

Hail occurs very infrequently but has recently defoliated the upper canopy of more than 100 hectares of forest in the Buffelsnek area north of Knysna. Winds cause the breakage of large branches or occasionally uproot a single tree, or at the most a small group of trees. Large windfalls occur very infrequently in the southern Cape and other forests along the Escarpment. In northern KwaZulu-Natal cyclones occasionally flatten

ABOVE At Noetzie, a tranquil river winds lazily among forested hills.

ABOVE The handsome rameron pigeon occurs widely in South African forests.

ABOVE The formidable crowned eagle is Africa's most powerful bird of prey.

large parts of the coastal forests. However, most trees die standing and singly from old age, or some form of disease or stress.

FOREST MICROCLIMATE

Mixed evergreen forest is a layered community, and always has a continuous tree stratum, with or without a shrub and/or a herbaceous stratum. The layering and the closed forest canopy buffer the outer macroclimate to create a more equable internal microclimate.

In the Groenkop forest near George, a tower was erected in a treefall gap in a forest with a canopy 22 metres high. Air temperature, air humidity and windspeed were measured above the main canopy at 25 metres, in the main canopy, in the less dense subcanopy layer above the shrub layer, and in the dense shrub layer at one metre above the ground. In relation to conditions above the canopy, the temperature in the shrub layer was lower, the humidity was higher and the wind speed was considerably lower to almost nonexistent, even during berg-wind conditions. The plants growing below the canopy are, therefore, adapted to these conditions, as well to the low light intensities. Tree seedlings starting their life cycle below the canopy gradually adapt to the altered, more extreme conditions as they grow into the canopy.

Large gaps created in the canopy during road construction or careless timber harvesting, have two major effects on the plants growing in and around such gaps. Below-canopy plants are exposed to the more extreme conditions prevailing outside the canopy. Many of them cannot adapt to the changed conditions, and die. Wind blowing over the relatively smooth, undulating forest canopy, becomes turbulent within the gap and uproots the trees on the side of the gap from which the wind blows.

Vegetation of a natural forest edge has an effect on the microclimate of the forest interior similar to that of the closed forest canopy. A natural forest edge consists of plants of various growth forms and sizes that close the gaps between the mature trees. It usually forms what is known as a soft edge, which gradually decreases in height and increases in foliage density away from the mature forest. The plants of the forest edge are adapted to the exterior, more extreme conditions, and often include species that only grow along the forest margin. This transitional area, or ecotone, also has a higher biodiversity than either the forest or the outside vegetation, because it includes elements of both.

Creation of a hard forest edge, such as during removal of the forest edge vegetation or cutting of a clearing in the forest, exposes the forest interior to penetration by the hot, dry, and gusty winds, to the detriment of the less hardy plant species that grow there.

NUTRIENT CYCLING

The high rainfall in areas where forests grow has two major effects on forest soils. It causes waterlogged conditions in clayey soils and leaches the soluble nutrients deeper into the soil. The result is that the trees develop very shallow root systems. Studies conducted in the southern Cape forests show that the root system of a tree has a maximum depth immediately beneath the bole, and decreases further away from the tree where the roots were confined to the top 30 centimetres of the soil.

Large individual trees of Outeniqua yellowwood (*Podocarpus falcatus*) have roots of more than 20 centimetres in diameter appearing above the soil surface and extending horizontally for distances in excess of 40 metres away from the bole.

ABOVE *The chorister robin is a South African forest endemic.*

ABOVE *A forest stream at Mount Sheba in Mpumalanga.*

A dense mat of fine, feeder roots is concentrated in the upper 10 centimetres of the soil, for two reasons. The waterlogged conditions inhibit their penetration deeper into the soil – they will suffocate from lack of oxygen. The main function of the feeder roots is to absorb nutrients from decomposing litter in the upper part of the soil profile. Very often, small roots colonise decomposing logs above the root mat and humus layer, thereby gaining rapid access to the nutrients they hold. This root mat is, therefore, one of the most important mechanisms for direct nutrient cycling and conservation in a rainforest. Disturbance of the root and litter layers will adversely affect forest regeneration and recovery.

In closed forests, shallow-rooted trees are supported by surrounding trees. When gaps or forest edges are created, the new edge trees are more prone to windfalls, especially when part of the root system is damaged or removed. The trees are also particularly sensitive to poor soil aeration caused by standing water resulting from disturbance of the natural drainage patterns, and from soil compaction.

The high nutrient content in the surface layers of soil is maintained through the fall of litter – leaves, twigs, bark, flowers and fruit – as well as through the death of forest animals.

Contrary to the general perception that leaves fall in autumn, leaf-fall in the evergreen forests occurs throughout the year, but with a definite peak in mid-summer (December and January). During this time the rainfall is high, but the trees experience a physiological drought due to the high temperatures and associated high loss of water due to transpiration (loss of water through the leaves of a plant).

Evergreen forest trees have developed a nutrient-conservation mechanism to cope with the characteristic nutrient-poor soils of their environment. During spring they flush new leaves and the nutrients are translocated within the tree from the old leaves to the new leaves. Only then, in mid-summer, are the old leaves dropped.

The total litter fall in forests in the southern Cape amounts to some 3 000 and 4 500 kilograms a hectare each year, and up to 10 000 kilograms per hectare per year in the higher rainfall areas of the forests in the Northern Province. The total amount of litter increases with increasing total mass of living material (biomass) of the forest, which again depends on the rainfall. The litter, of which the leaf component forms about 80 per cent, decomposes relatively quickly. The rate of decomposition is about two years for moist forest, and four years for dry forest, resulting in a gradual build-up of litter on the forest floor.

Forests can grow anywhere in any site, nutrient-poor or shallow soils, provided that the moisture is sufficient and disturbance is minimised, so that the closed nutrient cycle can develop. However, it is a slow process, and one that requires the recovery and increase of the nutrient status in the upper layers of the soil.

BIODIVERSITY, ENDEMISM AND SPECIES COMPOSITION

Forest species composition is the result of all the historical processes of migration, adaptation and speciation, together with life-cycle processes of seed dispersal, germination, seedling establishment, growth and mortality. It is also dependent on the on-site processes of competition, stress and disturbance. All species have developed through these processes, adapting accordingly in order to survive, and so differing in habitat requirements and tolerance ranges to adverse conditions.

ABOVE   Decomposition of fallen leaves and other forms of plant and animal litter maintains a high nutrient level in the surface layer of forest soil.

ABOVE   A shaft of sunlight penetrating a forest glade is captured in a spider web.
OPPOSITE   A cool mist invades a high-altitude forest.

Recent studies showed that the very small area of forest in South Africa (0.56 per cent of southern Africa) contains at least 1 500 species of flowering plants and ferns (7.1 per cent of all indigenous plant species in South Africa). The ratio of 0.58 species per square kilometre makes the forests the second richest biome per unit area in South Africa, after fynbos with 1.36 species per kilometre. Woody plants represent 50 per cent of the species, and include canopy trees (15 per cent), subcanopy trees (27 per cent), woody shrubs (47 per cent) and lianes (woody climbers) (11 per cent). The herbaceous growth forms include vines (17 per cent), terrestrial ferns (13 per cent), epiphytes, excluding mosses (8 per cent), geophytes (10 per cent), graminoids (13 per cent) and forbs (39 per cent). Epiphytes are plants that anchor themselves to grow on other plants – in order to obtain a more favourable position with regard to light – but which are not parasitic, such as orchids, ferns and mosses. Geophytes are bulbous plants, graminoids are grasslike plants, and forbs are all other herbaceous plants.

Afro-montane forests, in general, have less species than coastal and sand forests. Furthermore, drier, warmer forests are richer in species than wetter, cooler forests.

The forest with most plant species in South Africa – about 500 species – occurs in the Umtamvuna River Gorge between Transkei and KwaZulu-Natal, although it is a relatively small forest covering just over 1 000 hectares. The area is a meeting point of different plant dispersal corridors, which connect the mountain and coastal forests, and the substrate is a quartzitic sandstone, which is known to have a remarkably high number of endemic woody species. The second richest forest is the southern Cape forest complex with 465 species.

Some interesting patterns emerge when the floras of different forests are compared. Generally, forests share many more of their species with forests to their north or east than with forests to their south or west.

For example, the southern Cape forests share 63 per cent of its woody species with those of the Amatole forests, 56 per cent with the Umtamvuna forest and 43 per cent with the Mariepskop along the eastern

SEED AGE

*I*n the Witelsbos forest in the Tsitsikamma an abrupt change in the density and height of the understorey attracted my attention. On closer investigation, I discovered abundant pieces of charcoal and keur seed below the feeder roots. I concluded that the forest must have been destroyed by fire some time ago, and that the fire stimulated keur seed to germinate and to develop into a nurse stand. Over time forest species such as stinkwood, yellowwood, and several others of the present forest canopy would have established themselves, eventually replacing the shade-intolerant keur. From stem sections of the Outeniqua yellowwood (Podocarpus falcatus) taken from a road clearing in the same area, I managed to determine the age of the trees, and hence the minimum period since the fire. My calculations indicated that the fire had occurred some 230 years ago, making the keur seed at least that old, and still viable, waiting for the next devastating fire to repeat its cycle!

Several such berg-wind driven fires burnt through the Tsitsikamma between 1996 and 1999, and burnt through part of Klein Witelsbos forest. The keur seed from the soil-stored seed banks in this forest germinated in mass – to start the recovery process.

Escarpment, but only 40 per cent with the nearby Grootvadersbosch near Swellendam, about 200 kilometres to the west.

In the reverse order, Grootvadersbosch shares 95 per cent, the Amatole forests 61 per cent, the Umtamvuna forest 30 per cent and the Mariepskop forests 40 per cent of their woody species with the southern Cape forests.

This relates to the so-called erosion of species from the tropical source areas, southwards to the southwestern Cape forests.

Many coastal forest plant species drop out from north to south along the northern KwaZulu-Natal coastal areas. A study in the southern Cape has shown that 206 of the 465 forest species reach their distribution limits within the southern Cape forests, mostly from the east, or have disjunct distributions within those forests and wider distributions outside, again mostly to the east. Most of these patterns can be related to environmental change over thousands or even millions of years.

For example, north of Knysna a large, viable population of terblans (*Faurea macnaughtonii*), a forest canopy tree of the protea family, grows in isolation. Outside of this stand, the nearest population of terblans occurs in Egossa forest in the Eastern Cape, and isolated populations occur in Nkandhla forest in KwaZulu-Natal, in Mariepskop forest, in the Usambara mountain forest in Tanzania, and in Madagascar.

In Nature's Valley east of Plettenberg Bay, isolated but viable populations of Cape teak (*Strychnos decussata*) exist; its nearest neighbours are found near Port Elizabeth. Cape wild banana (*Strelitzia alba*) is an endemic, and its closest relatives occur near East London, while false horsewood (*Hippobromus pauciflorus*) has its nearest neighbours near Humansdorp.

In the Bitou River valley between Plettenberg Bay and Nature's Valley, several species such as the forest boer-bean tree (*Schotia latifolia*), shrubs, such as the Cape laburnum (*Calpurnia aurea*) and sysel bush (*Plumbago auriculata*), a jasmine climber (*Jasminum angulare*), a vine (*Vernonia anisochaetoides*) and various forbs (*Aptenia cordifolia* and *Plectranthus madagascariensis*) grow in isolation in the dry scrub forest. The interesting patterns in this area are related to the spread of these species along the lowlands south of the present coastline, when the sea level was much further south during the Glacial Period of 18 000 years ago. When, about 9 000 years ago, the sea level took on its present position, these populations were cut off and isolated from the other populations situated to the east. There are many other similarly interesting examples.

Growth form composition, canopy height and degree of layering vary along the environmental gradients of moisture, temperature, nutrient status, and disturbance regime within different forest areas. In combination, they form the forest types that are closely related to the different landscape zones.

ABOVE A small pocket of forest in a steep river valley in the Drakensberg.

KNYSNA FERN

*L*eaves (fronds) of the Knysna or seven weeks fern (Rumohra adiantiformis) are used extensively in the florist trade, both locally and abroad. It is a protected plant that is harvested from the southern Cape forests, but is currently also cultivated in nurseries or underneath thinned pine stands. Scientific studies have provided a basis for its sustained harvesting from the forest. Ecologically the frequency of frond harvesting and quality of the fronds are controlled by the internal cycling of nutrients, in particular potassium, through the plant. The size, moisture content and life period of the mature frond is controlled by the potassium reserves in the plant. The potassium content is high in the growing tip and unfolding frond, and as the frond ages, the potassium is recycled to the growing tip. Too-frequent harvesting of the mature fronds reduces the potassium in the growing tip and causes a reduction in size and quality of newly developing fronds. The commercialisation of this indigenous, protected plant has definitely contributed to a better study of the species, and to conservation of the species and the small forest patches on farms which otherwise would be cleared.

For example, in the southern Cape, the mountain and foothill forests are mostly wet to moist high forests with an abundance of ferns, few tree species, and few epiphytes, and few climbers. The coastal platform forests are moist to dry, high forests with a high richness of species of trees, shrubs and epiphytes, and variable numbers of climbers, ferns, graminoids and forbs. The scrub forests and dry, high forests of the coastal scarp and steep slopes of river valleys have a high species richness of trees, shrubs, climbers, geophytes and forbs, variable numbers of epiphytes and grasses, and very few ferns. They contain many thorny shrubs, deciduous trees and climbers.

WILDLIFE

Most of the mammals and a large proportion of the birds found in South African forests are not confined to the forest habitat and have wide distribution ranges.

Forest mammals generally occur solitarily or in small groups, are shy and many are nocturnal. Special techniques are needed to study them. In Goudveld forest near Knysna auto-triggering cameras were used over a six-month period to record 13 mammal species in six one-square-kilometre census blocks.

Amongst the larger mammals found in South Africa's evergreen forest areas are bushbuck (*Tragelaphus scriptus*), bushpig (*Potamochoerus porcus*), blue duiker (*Cephalophus monticola*), baboon (*Papio ursinus*), vervet monkey (*Cercopithecus pygerythrus*), leopard (*Panthera pardus*), and fruit bats such as the Egyptian fruit bat (*Rousettus aegyptiacus*).

Bird species richness is relatively low in forest areas, and decline from north to south in a similar pattern to the plant species. For example, moving southwards from the Eastern Cape, 54 species have been recorded in Dwesa forest, 43 in Alexandria forest, 35 in Diepwalle forest near Knysna, and only 15 in forest patches of the Cape Peninsula.

Birds endemic to southern African forests and thicket include such attractive and interesting species as the Knysna lourie (*Tauraco corythaix*), Knysna woodpecker (*Campethera notata*), bush blackcap (*Lioptilus nigricapillus*), chorister robin (*Cossypha dichroa*), brown robin (*Erythropygia signata*), southern tchagra (*Tchagra tchagra*), and the forest canary (*Serinus scotops*). However, the majority of birds occurring in South African forests occur in forested regions further north as well.

These include the fruit-eating rameron pigeon (*Columba arquatrix*) and sombre bulbul (*Andropadus importunus*); sallying insectivores such as the Narina trogon (*Apaloderma narina*), starred robin (*Pogonocichla stellata*), Cape batis (*Batis capensis*), and paradise flycatcher (*Terpsiphone viridis*); foliage gleaning insectivores such as Cape white-eye (*Zosterops pallidus*), puffback shrike (*Dryoscopus cubla*), and yellow-throated warbler (*Seicercus ruficapillus*); bark gleaning insectivores that include the olive woodpecker (*Mesopicos griseocephalus*) and red-billed hoopoe (*Phoeniculus purpureus*); ground-gleaning insect-eaters such as the olive thrush (*Turdus olivaceus*) and the terrestrial bulbul (*Phyllastrephus terrestris*); ground-feeding seedeaters, for example the cinnamom dove (*Aplopelia larvata*); and nectar-feeding species such as the lesser double-collared sunbird (*Nectarinia chalybea*).

INTERACTIONS OF IMPORTANT PLANT SPECIES

Management systems for sustained utilisation of forest species should be based on a thorough understanding of the ecology of the particular species, and of the communities in which the species grow. Studies of various species have shown the intricate relationships between plants, animals, site conditions and physiological processes in the plants.

Black stinkwood is a well-known furniture timber tree, and its bark is extensively used in traditional medicine. The species is closely related to imbuia (*Ocotea porosa*) – a furniture timber tree of the Brazilian sub-tropical rainforests – and to the camphor tree (*Tarchonanthus* spp.), and to trees of the Lauraceae family, such as avocado pear and laurel. In the mountain forests of the southern Cape it forms about 30 per cent of the stems, but the area is very inaccessible for timber harvesting. Timber is mainly cut from the coastal platform forests where the tree forms only one to four per cent of the stems. The species grows in moister sites and is very sensitive to changes in the drainage system. An indigenous pathogenic fungus, *Phytophthora cinnamomi*, causes root rotting and crown die-back during wet conditions, especially after inappropriate harvesting practices have compacted the soil and created water-logged conditions.

ABOVE The Lone Creek waterfall plummets into a forest pool near Sabie.

ABOVE The outer branches of tall forest trees are often draped in old man's beard, a lichen.

ABOVE Below a moss-covered fallen tree trunk, a seed larder betrays the presence of a forest rodent.

Fortunately, the tree has developed the ability to resprout from the stem base when stressed, or when damaged by fire or lightning. It is therefore important to manage the coppice shoots that develop on the stump after harvesting, particularly because these young shoots are browsed by bushbuck. A coppice shoot utilises the established root system, and can grow to a mature tree in about 100 years compared to the 400 to 500 years a tree would require to grow to the same size from seed. This coppicing ability has also contributed to the persistence of the tree under the uncontrolled, excessive harvesting of stinkwood between 1750 and 1930 in the Knysna area.

South African yellowwoods (*Podocarpus* species) form part of the largest conifer group in the Southern Hemisphere – the podocarps.

CONSERVATION

Forest complexes in South Africa are generally well conserved, either in private and tribal owned conservancies that are in good condition, or in natural heritage sites, nature reserves and wilderness areas proclaimed under the Forest Act. There are many privately owned and communal forests outside of proclaimed areas that are well conserved, but have insecure conservation status. Ownership determines the type and quality of forest management and possible impacts on the vegetation. Governments in the region manage and control the largest forests and a very big part of the total forest area. A relatively small portion are privately owned. However, in KwaZulu-Natal many forests are on private land, but the Conservancy System and the Natural Heritage System contribute to forest conservation. It is noteworthy that controlled utilisation of reserved trees and ferns on private land through a permit system contributed to forest conservation in many areas.

Pressure is still exerted on indigenous forests by the growing needs of the increasing populations in rural areas; high intensity farming interests – such as in the Eastern Cape lowlands – which cause the clearing of scrub forest for agriculture; economic pressures – which cause uncontrolled exploitation, grazing and burning of forests on farms; and developments of infrastructure and townships and coastal resorts.

After maltreatment for nearly two centuries, the remaining forests are at present in a relatively good condition, and are expanding in many areas. Sustained-use management forms the basis of resource utilisation from the largest forest complex in South Africa. Efforts are coordinated to expand this approach to different levels of forest size and management expertise.

Disturbance is a key factor in the maintenance of viable populations of many of the species – some need more of it, others less. Pioneer-type species are well represented in rural and other regularly disturbed areas with secondary forest (early development stages). They could become rare in many areas following protection and the progression of stand development towards maturity (late development stages). It is a challenge to reserve managers to maintain a balance between areas of early, middle and late forest development stages to maintain maximum species diversity.

Conservation of the forests require the maintenance of components and critical processes within a forest ecosystem, and maintenance of gene flow between the different forests. It is as much dependent on the sustained utilisation of the forest products as it is dependent on management of land surrounding the forest. The large ratio of forest margin to forest area accentuates the importance of forest margins to forest survival.

There are more than 100 species, of which only four occur in South Africa. The Breede River yellowwood (*Podocarpus elongatus*) is endemic to the southwestern Cape, and Henkel's yellowwood (*P. henkellii*) has a disjunct distribution in the montane forests from the Eastern Cape through KwaZulu-Natal to East Africa.

The upright or real yellowwood (*P. latifolius*) and the Outeniqua yellowwood are both widespread in the forests of southern and East Africa. The upright yellowwood is, however, far more common, forming 15 to 20 per cent of the stems in the southern Cape forests. The Outeniqua yellowwood forms only one per cent of the stems.

The key difference in stem numbers is to be found in fruit structures of the two species, which relate to the way the seed is dispersed. The fruit of the upright yellowwood consists of a pea-sized seed with leathery covering, which grows on a large blackish-purple, fleshy receptacle. Large birds, such as the Knysna lourie, eat the fleshy receptacle and disperse the seed, which then germinates within two months.

The fruit of the Outeniqua yellowwood consists of a similar-sized seed covered by a woody shell, which in turn is surrounded by a yellow, fleshy pulp. The Egyptian fruit bat is the main disperser. It chews the fleshy pulp from the seed, discards the seed, sucks the juice from the pulp, and then discards the chewed pulp. It has been suggested that the hard shell developed to protect the seed against the teeth of the bat.

The consequence of this adaptation is that germination is delayed for about 12 months. In this period forest rodents collect and eat the seed, and thus prevent seedlings from becoming established. The few trees that do become established have a further problem in that the trees are either male or female, like all podocarps. This has an adverse effect on the viability of the seed in sparse populations.

It is therefore important to consider the sex of the Outeniqua yellowwood when trees are harvested. It is also interesting to note that the Outeniqua yellowwood grows about twice as fast as the upright yellowwood. An Outeniqua tree that measures one metre in diameter

ABOVE A wild date palm in a dark patch of coastal forest.

ABOVE Ferns are primitive plants that do not bear flowers.

will be about 400 years old, whereas an upright of the same size will be approximately 750 years old.

A fleshy fruit is the most common fruit type in the tree species, and most of the larger fruits belong to canopy trees of the mature forest, such as the yellowwoods and stinkwood. Very few trees in the evergreen forest have dry fruits and long-living seeds.

One example is the keur tree (*Virgilia divaricata*), an endemic that grows as a pioneer on the forest margin in the southern Cape. The dark-brown seeds require heat – which is absent in undisturbed forest

– to initiate germination. Soil-stored seed banks are built up over years and such seed only germinates after hot fires, such as those that occur during the hot, devastating berg winds.

Knowledge of the 'nursing process' of pioneer species (see 'seed age' box on page 120) is important in forest conservation, as by imitating nature and introducing trees such as the keur to cleared areas, or to manage stands of invader plants such as Australian blackwood (*Acacia melanoxylon*, and black wattle (*A. mearnsii*), and pines and eucalypts, it is possible to convert these stands to indigenous forest.

Many tree species were introduced into South Africa to supplement the indigenous species to satisfy the increasing demand for timber. Some of these introduced species were then able to invade neighbouring grasslands and shrublands where the naturally occurring fire regime was excluded to protect the timber investments. Fortunately most of the introduced pines, eucalypts, wattle and other invader plants are intolerant of shade and cannot spread in well-managed indigenous forest. For example, the alien Australian blackwood has been planted since the turn of the nineteenth century in the large gaps left by excessive felling in the forest. Today blackwood forms the bulk of the timber that is annually cut from the southern Cape forests, along with the yellowwoods, stinkwood and other indigenous species. Blackwood can only establish outside on the forest margin where dense stands are formed. These stands are manipulated through thinning to enable indigenous species to become established, as they would do with keur, as a nurse stand.

FOREST USES

The recognition of the products and values of forests is one of the basic requirements in order to reduce conflicts in land-use options and to conserve forests.

Forests have always provided for the subsistence needs of rural people in respect of construction material and fuel. A variety of tree species are used for building materials, depending on style and availability of materials, but it is not only the forest timber that is used, as climbers, leaves, leaf petioles and tree bark are also valuable sources of binding materials. Wood for fuel is gathered from indigenous forests where there are no alternatives, such as eucalypt or wattle plantations or woodlots.

Climbers are used extensively in the craft industry, mainly in the making of baskets, which, for example, forms an important part of the local economy and traditions of the Pondo people around Port St Johns in the Eastern Cape.

Traditional medicines are important to rural communities for medical, psychosomatic and economic reasons.

Forest plants – including trees, shrubs, climbers, epiphytes and parasites – and even forest-dwelling animals – particularly millipedes, baboons, genets and snakes are used by rural people in the making of

ABOVE A cinnamon dove rests quietly on the forest floor.

traditional medicines, or *muti*. The urban demand for traditional medicines has generated a huge trade between rural source areas and the urban market, often with devastating consequences for the forests in rural areas.

Fruits, wild spinach, honey and edible fungi provide important dietary supplements to rural people in less developed areas of South Africa, providing nutrients deficient in their starchy staple diet. Such exploitation is increased during drought periods, particularly in areas with marginal agricultural potential. Afro-montane forest is generally poor in edible-fruit-bearing species, whereas coastal forest and sand forest areas of northern KwaZulu-Natal have the highest diversity of fruit-bearing species.

Forests also have cultural importance. The burial site at Thathe forest is of cultural importance to the Vhavenda people, as is the burial site of Dingaan in Hlatikulu forest to the Zulu people. Undisturbed forest and wooded copses persist around major grave sites in many parts of southern Africa, due to the importance attached by the local people to the role of ancestral spirits in their daily lives and in ensuring them peace.

Only the southern Cape forests and parts of the Amatole forests are today subjected to scientific planning and management for sustained resource harvesting. Furniture timber and fern leaves are used conservatively from ecologically suitable but small areas of forest. The single-tree selection system for harvesting timber trees provides for the maintenance of the ecological processes in the forest. The crowns of large utilisable trees are removed before felling the bole in order to reduce damage to the canopy, to keep gap size in accordance with the natural disturbance regime. Special care is taken to minimise soil compaction and drainage disturbance during extraction of the timber. Under special circumstances helicopters are used to lift logs of valuable species from sensitive sites.

Forests play an increasingly important role in providing recreation and aesthetics for the growing urbanised and industrialised societies of southern Africa.

The availability of such recreation areas is important not only for the burgeoning tourist industry, but as a tool in conservation education.

DROUGHT

The effects of a severe, cyclic drought were studied in the Eastern Cape forests. The leaves of most evergreen trees died on the trees. The leaves of the evergreen boxwood (Buxus macowanii) remained green throughout the drought, but many plants died shortly afterwards when they were totally defoliated by larvae of a moth species, which appeared in large numbers after the first rains. The deciduous sneezewood (Ptaeroxylon obliquum) lost its leaves during the drought, and responded very quickly after the rains by flushing new leaves, flowering and shedding of seeds soon afterwards. The sneezewood seedlings benefited from the gaps caused by the dying boxwood trees.

Fynbos

Dave Richardson

South Africa's fynbos biome forms part of the Cape Floristic Region (CFR), and covers about 71 300 square kilometres. The fynbos is home to more than 7 300 species of plants – about 45 per cent of the flora of southern Africa crammed into about four per cent of its surface area. Almost 80 per cent of the plant species that grow in the fynbos biome are endemic to the region. The CFR is recognised as one of the world's six plant kingdoms, and South Africa is the only country that contains an entire floral kingdom within its boundaries, making it one of the biodiversity giants of the world.

Fynbos is the name given to the predominant vegetation of the mountains and coastal lowlands of the Western Cape Province, and the Eastern Cape Province west of Port Elizabeth. The term was first used by Dutch settlers, who referred to the shrubby vegetation on Table Mountain and the adjacent countryside as *'fijnbosch'* – alluding either to the dominance of fine or small-leaved shrubs in the vegetation, or perhaps to the poor potential of its slender timber as a forestry resource.

For many years fynbos was known in scientific circles as macchia, which is the anglicised name of the structurally similar *maquis* shrublands in southern France. The term fynbos, however, is now firmly entrenched in both scientific and popular literature, and has been assimilated as part of the natural heritage of South Africa. The term fynbos may be understood in a narrow sense – where it refers to the shrubland vegetation described above, or in a wider sense – applying to the entire region where fynbos is the predominant and characteristic vegetation type. This latter term encompasses the mountains and coastal lowlands from Niewoudtville in the northwest to the Cape Peninsula in the southwest, and to Port Elizabeth in the southeast. This region is the fynbos biome, which includes 'true' fynbos and renosterveld (a shrubland on clay-like soils) vegetation types, as well as patches of Afro-montane forest, and various types of thicket. Majestic mountains and a spectacular coastline make this an area of great scenic diversity and beauty, in many parts still uniquely 'wild' in character. The area is characterised by

FROM LEFT TO RIGHT Leucadendron eucalyptifolium; *A total of 657* Erica *species are known to occur in South Africa; An abundance of life emerges in the aftermath of a fire. However, many fynbos plants are killed by fire, and rely entirely on seed banks for reproduction;* Leucospermum cordifolium.
BELOW The shimmering silver tree, conspicuous at Wynberg and Kirstenbosch, is a rare and localised Leucadendron *of the mountains of the Cape Peninsula.*

hot, dry summers, high winds, and the two factors that are of overriding importance in fynbos communities: recurring, intense fires, and low-nutrient soils.

VEGETATION TYPES

Fynbos includes both true fynbos and renosterveld vegetation types.

True fynbos vegetation types

These cover approximately 41 650 square kilometres. The most extensive of these, montane fynbos, is also the best preserved because of the inaccessibility of its habitat – the majestic Cape mountains. Other types are limited to specific substrates. Thus the sand plain fynbos is confined to the deep, acid soils of the west coast; laterite fynbos to lateritic, seasonally waterlogged soils; and limestone fynbos to calcareous, alkaline, shallow soils along the south coast. Grassy fynbos occurs in areas to the east where summer rainfall increases. Here grasses typical of the grassland biome replace the restioid component of typical fynbos.

Renosterveld vegetation types

Central mountain renosterveld is confined to the montane areas on the fringes of the Little and Great Karoo basins, often situated between fynbos and Karoo vegetation types. Escarpment mountain renosterveld occurs on the slopes and foothills of the western parts of the Great Escarpment. Northwestern mountain renosterveld is confined to the Kamiesberg highlands. It merges with the succulent karoo at lower and fynbos at higher altitudes. West Coast renosterveld is found on the lowlands of the West Coast. Only three per cent of the natural vegetation of this veld type still exists. Accordingly, a large number of endangered plant species occur in the area. South and southwest coast renosterveld differs from other renosterveld types in having a very high proportion of grasses.

ORIGINS

About 60 million years ago, forests dominated by palm trees and yellowwoods covered much of the Cape coastal lowlands, persisting until some three million years ago, when the climate at the Cape changed rapidly from tropical to temperate, and eventually to what it is today: a mediterranean-type climate with winter rainfall and dry summers.

This phase of increasing aridity heralded the extinction of many forest plants. An important repercussion of the drier conditions was the increased incidence of fire. Frequent fires caused the demise of most tropical plants in the region, and set in motion the selective forces that formed the fynbos life forms evident today. Ancestors of the plants that now dominate fynbos communities were found predominantly at high altitudes and in other situations that were unsuitable or suboptimal for the growth of the tropical forest species. These plants spread as

conditions became drier and fires were more frequent, filling the gaps vacated by the tropical species. The diversity of the landscapes into which they spread, as well as other environmental factors, promoted a rapid proliferation of species – a process known as speciation. The fynbos region, effectively an 'island' of nutrient-poor soils at the southwestern tip of Africa, was thus isolated from other evolving floras. Fire and nutrient-poor soils became the major driving forces in the evolution of the extraordinary assemblage of plants that now comprise fynbos communities.

COMPOSITION

Generally, true fynbos is a shrubland characterised by a unique mixture of three main plant types or growth forms: proteoid, ericoid and restioid.

Proteoids include the broad, leathery-leaved shrubs of the Proteaceae family. Usually they are the tallest plants in the vegetation and the most

ABOVE A priceless fynbos heritage is conserved in the Cape of Good Hope Nature Reserve.

ABOVE Back-lit by brilliant late afternoon sunlight, Bulbinella latifolia *var.* doloritica *inflorescences glow like little lanterns. This orange form is entirely restricted to a small area near Nieuwoudtville.*

ABOVE Due to nutrient-poor foliage, larger mammals are not well-represented in fynbos regions. However, smaller mammals such as the dassie (rock hyrax) populate the rocky slopes of the mountains and even the coastline.

conspicuous, especially when the veld is coloured with their showy flowers. The concentration of Proteaceae species in the Western Cape Province contributes greatly to the general appearance of fynbos, and is probably its best-known feature. Ericoid plants, which form the lower shrub layer in fynbos, are heath-like and have small leaves. The group includes members of the species-rich genera *Erica*, *Aspalathus*, *Agathosma* and *Phylica*.

The combination of proteoid and ericoid shrubs alone is not the distinguishing mark of fynbos, as other shrublands in montane areas of Africa, for example in the KwaZulu-Natal Drakensberg, also have these elements. However, the feature that does characterise fynbos is the presence of the restioid (or Cape reed) growth form. All restioids belong to the Restionaceae family, which is found on most fragments of the former supercontinent of Gondwana (Australia, New Zealand and South America among them). However, restioids are most diverse and abundant in the Western Cape Province of South Africa.

Geophytes (herbs with underground storage organs such as bulbs, corms, rhizomes and tubers) are also an integral part of fynbos. There are about 3 000 geophytic species in the fynbos – the richest concentration of this growth form in the world. Some species flower in profusion after fires, creating spectacular displays that colour whole mountainsides or marshes. Many fynbos geophytes, including species of *Freesia*, *Gladiolus*, *Sparaxis* and *Watsonia*, all members of the iris family, are cultivated in gardens around the world.

Although large forests occur along the eastern coast of the Western Cape, west of Knysna the forest pockets disperse in size and species

richness. In fact, trees are not a characteristic element of fynbos and are absent from many such communities. The few tree species that are found in some fynbos areas are worthy of mention. The common mountain cedar (*Widdringtonia nodiflora*) is found throughout the region, and sometimes forms small, dense thickets. The Clanwilliam cedar (*W. cederbergensis*) is a conspicuous and characteristic element of the Cederberg range. Several other tree species, notably the mountain maytenus (*Maytenus oleoides*) and the rockwood (*Heeria argentea*) are more widespread in fynbos areas, but are confined to rocky sites that afford them protection from fire. Patches of forest with true forest trees such as the rooiels (*Cunonia capensis*) and the real yellowwood (*Podocarpus latifolius*), are usually confined to boulder screes and deep kloofs. Although tree seedlings do establish in fynbos, they are destroyed by the frequent fires that perpetuate the predominance of fire-adapted shrubs.

All renosterveld types occur on fine-grained soils, fertile clay and silt derived from shales. Renosterveld is characterised by members of the daisy family, and is dominated by renosterbos (*Elytropappus rhinocerotis*). Proteas, ericas and restios, all typical of fynbos, are rare in renosterveld. Grasses are abundant, but overgrazing has promoted the increase of renosterbos at the expense of the grass layer.

INTERNATIONAL AFFINITIES OF FYNBOS AND THE MEDITERRANEAN-TYPE CLIMATE

The fynbos biome shares certain features with other areas of the world which have a mediterranean-type climate, defined as a semiarid regime with cool, wet winters and hot, dry summers. (Because the southern and

ABOVE   A cave in the Cederberg range.

RIGHT   Contorted rock strata in Meiringspoort in the Swartberg bear testimony to the titanic earth movements that gave birth to the Cape Fold Mountains.

eastern fynbos regions also receive summer rains, only the southwestern tip is considered to be a true mediterranean-type ecosystem. Such ecosystems include the Mediterranean Basin, the coastal areas of California, central Chile, and southeastern and southwestern Australia. The mediterranean-type shrublands are known by different names in different parts of the world: *garrigue*, *maquis* and *phrygana* in the Mediterranean Basin, chaparral in California, *matorral* in Chile and *kwongan* in Western Australia.

Common features in mediterranean-type ecosystems are a relatively low rate of plant growth, the predominance of sclerophyllous shrubs (those with tough, thick, evergreen leaves), and regular fires during the hot, dry summer/autumn periods. The mediterranean-type climate was more prevalent in the Pleistocene Period (more than 12 000 years ago), an important factor in the evolution of fynbos life forms. Even in the western part of the South African fynbos region, many areas, especially in the mountains, receive too much rainfall to be truly 'mediterranean'. For example, the Dwarsberg Plateau in the mountains between Stellenbosch and Villiersdorp receives up to 3 600 millimetres of rain a year, the highest recorded annual rainfall in southern Africa.

East of the Breede River, the rainfall is distributed fairly evenly over the year, and the easternmost part of the biome, near Port Elizabeth, receives at least half its rainfall in summer. Fynbos is clearly not restricted to areas with a mediterranean-type climate.

Rather, it is soil type, together with complex interactions between climate and fire (see box on page 140), that is paramount in determining where fynbos grows.

ABOVE The Bontebok National Park was specifically proclaimed to conserve the beautifully marked bontebok.

BELOW The exquisite little orange-breasted sunbird is a fynbos endemic. It is particularly fond of the flowers of the Erica genus.

TYPICAL FYNBOS LANDSCAPE

The rugged and dissected nature of the Cape landscape contributes considerably to the scenic beauty and wilderness character of the fynbos biome. Parallel series of steep mountains run north to south along the west coast, and west to east along the south coast. The main ranges are separated by long valleys, and there is a relatively narrow coastal plain. These topographical features have a significant influence on the organisms of the fynbos biome as they provide a great variety of habitats for plants and animals. The pattern of peaks and valleys, slopes and plateaux also creates dramatic differences in microclimate. Fynbos protects the steep mountain slopes against erosion. Furthermore, fynbos is remarkably frugal in its use of water so that, as water catchment areas, the fynbos-clad Cape mountains are highly efficient.

The role of the landscape and soil in determining the structure and composition of the plant and animal communities in fynbos biota can be traced back to a time some 900 million years ago, when the area now known as the fynbos biome lay at the edge of an inland sea. Thick deposits of mud and sand accumulated on the slope between the shallow ocean basins and the continental shelf. These deposits eventually hardened to form the shales of the Malmesbury beds.

About 500 million years ago, massive movements of the earth's crust caused buckling, folding and faulting of the Malmesbury beds. Melted rock (magma) welled up from deep within the earth's core and was pushed into, and sometimes over, these beds. The magma later crystallised to become Cape granite. During the next 50 million years, this complex mixture of rocks was slowly uplifted and eroded to become a flat, featureless plain. This plain in turn subsided beneath the sea to form the floor of a shallow basin. Over the following 50 million years, sand and fine mud were deposited in the basin to become the sediments of the Cape Supergroup. First to be deposited were the sandstones of the Table Mountain Group. Next came the shales and sandstones – first those of the Bokkeveld Group, then those of the Witteberg Group.

Rocks of these groups, named after the mountains where they were first recorded, were the building blocks of the fynbos landscape.

The accident of geological history that resulted in the formation of these rock types in what was to become the fynbos biome had profound implications for the life forms inhabiting its contrasting sandy and clay-like origins. About 250 million years ago, earth movements uplifted and buckled the sediments of the Table Mountain Group, causing them to rise some 6 000 metres out of the sea and heralding the birth of the Cape Fold Mountains. Erosion slowly reduced these mountains to their present forms, which are, by comparison, little more than high hills of resistant sandstone with a maximum elevation of 2 325 metres at Seweweekspoort peak in the Klein Swartberg. Weathering and other soil-forming processes gave rise to the present-day complex arrangement of soils.

ABOVE *The shadows of clouds shift silently over the Wolfberg, a peak high in the Cederberg range.*

Mountain soils are derived from sandstone or mixtures of sandstone and granite; they are acidic and extremely poor in essential nutrients, notably nitrogen and phosphorus. Soils in the lowlands, mainly derived from shales, are more fertile. The coastal plain has a complex sequence of inland acidic sands and coastal alkaline sands of marine and aeolian (wind-deposited) origin. As conditions became drier and fire frequency increased, the ancestors of current fynbos species began to fill the gaps left by receding tropical species. As a result, these new colonists were confronted by a complex topography and arrangement of soils.

The processes of speciation and reordering that ensued to forge the species-rich communities were complex, and are not yet fully understood. We can, however, get some idea of what happened by looking at the patterns of endemism in the flora.

ENDEMISM

The fynbos flora has, by global standards, an unusually high number of endemics. Many of them are confined to very limited areas, often as small as a few square kilometres.

THREATS TO THE FYNBOS

Major threats include urbanisation, the spread of vigorous alien plants such as pines, hakeas and wattles, too frequent fires, and over-harvesting of wild flowers. All these factors adversely affect the bio-diversity and aesthetic appeal of fynbos. In many areas, fynbos has been replaced by dense thickets of alien plants with a much greater biomass than fynbos. Aside from causing a reduction in biodiversity by suppressing indigenous species, this dramatic change in vegetation structure reduces water yield from catchments by up to half. Water is already a major limiting factor for economic development in the region, and further reductions are inevitable if alien plants are permitted to spread further.

Solutions to conservation problems such as fire management in areas with alien plants, and management of rare species and fragments of natural vegetation must take ecological and practical considerations into account. Properly managed fynbos is not only an irreplaceable asset of cultural value, but also an invaluable economic resource. South Africa cannot afford to lose it.

ABOVE *In the Cape Floristic Region, more plants can be found per square metre than anywhere else on earth.*

Fynbos endemics can be divided into two groups: the palaeoendemics that belong to ancient plant groups, only distantly related to most of the existing flora; and the neoendemics (a group to which the majority of fynbos endemics belong), that evolved more recently and have close living relatives in the existing flora.

Of the 150 fynbos families of the Cape flora, the 15 largest contain almost 70 per cent of the flora, and of the 950 genera, the 10 largest contain more than 20 per cent of the flora. Each of these 10 genera has more than 100 species, namely *Erica* (526), *Aspalathus* (245), *Ruschia* (138, many of them in the succulent Karoo), *Phylica* (133), *Agathosma* (130), *Oxalis* (129), *Pelargonium* (125), *Senecio* (113), *Cliffortia* (106) and *Muraltia* (106).

The extraordinary species-richness in fynbos is obviously not evenly distributed between families and genera; speciation has been much more prolific in some plant groups than in others.

Many endemic fynbos plants are dwarf, small-leaved shrubs that are killed by fire and produce relatively few, but large seeds. These plant species rely entirely on their meagre and short-lived seed banks – seeds

However, owing to a quirk of genetics, species that undergo population crashes are susceptible to the development of new genetic structure. This leads ultimately to the formation of new species, a process that is thought to have contributed greatly to the inordinate richness of plant species in fynbos.

Some distinguishable features are associated with this propensity to generate new species.

For example, many fynbos species, and most fynbos endemics, are adapted to grow only on specific soils – these species are termed edaphic specialists. This indicates the importance of soil as a selective force.

Alkaline substrata (notably limestone and calcareous sands) cover relatively small areas of the fynbos biome, but have exceptionally high levels of endemism, as is evident on the Agulhas Plain, where at least 110 endemic plant species grown on the Bredasdorp limestone formation. The large assortment of soil types in the biome provides a complex template that has kept speciating groups apart.

There are thus many habitat specialists, many of them with very small distribution ranges.

As a result, landscapes in the fynbos biome with a variety of geographical features separated by relatively short distances, have few species in common.

This rapid turnover of species over relatively short distances allows many species to be packed into the fynbos biome. It is this 'species packing' that makes fynbos unique in the world.

FAUNA

The fauna of the fynbos biome is not as extraordinary as its flora, and many visitors to fynbos regions are surprised by the seeming scarcity of animals. Indeed there are fewer animals, at least those of the big-and-hairy kind, in fynbos than in the other terrestrial biomes of South Africa. The reasons for this are complex.

Firstly, animals are mobile and can move in and out of the fynbos biome as they need to. The fynbos fauna, therefore, has not been as effectively isolated as the plant life, and animal species from adjacent biomes have also invaded fynbos. Thus the possibilities for animal speciation have been reduced.

Couple this with the fact that if nutrient deficiency, recurrent fires, and summer droughts pose big problems for plants, they present even greater problems for animals, especially those that are large and warm-blooded and need a constant supply of food.

Nutrient-deficient soils give rise to nutrient-poor foliage. The scarcity of nutritious food and intense fires mean that animals resident in fynbos must have special adaptations to find and exploit the sparse resources. To survive in fynbos areas, an animal would have to be small, occur in groups, and be a selective (specialised) feeder.

stored in the soil – for recruitment after fire. Furthermore, seeds of many endemic species are carried only short distances by their dispersers – mainly ants. A number of endemics occur only in small populations (more than 1 300 species, or 18 per cent of the fynbos flora, have such small populations that they are listed as threatened in the Red Data Book). Endemics are, quite obviously, highly vulnerable to population crashes. This may happen if an area burns only a few years after the previous fire, or at an unfavourable time of year (outside of summer/ autumn), or if rodents consume the entire seed crop.

For these reasons, large mammals are not well represented in the fynbos biome, and their role in the ecosystem is not as important as it is in grassland or savanna. The few large mammals that do occur are almost all specialised feeders.

They have anatomical, behaviourial and physiological adaptations that allow them to exist in small numbers, and to locate, eat and digest nutritious food that is not only scarce in general, but that is widely scattered in space and time.

Most vegetation in the fynbos biome has extremely low forage value; the leaves of many plants are tough and leathery, and chemical compounds make some species unpalatable.

The most common and widespread antelopes in the Cape mountains are the grysbok (*Raphicerus melanotis*) and the klipspringer (*Oreotragus oreotragus*). Both species are browsers, and feed mainly on palatable leaves, fruit, seed pods and flowers – which are scarce resources in many fynbos areas. Pairs, solitary individuals, or small family groups may be seen fairly regularly in fynbos.

Other antelopes, such as the endemic bontebok (*Damaliscus dorcas dorcas*), and Cape mountain zebra (*Equus zebra zebra*) are predominantly grazers. They occur in bigger groups than the grysbok and klipspringer, and are much more reliant on large tracts of vegetation. In the past they moved over great distances in search of nourishment, as did many other large mammals that are now extinct in the biome, including elephant (*Loxodonta africana*) and black rhinoceros (*Diceros bicornis*).

Forage is provided by post-fire flushes of sprouting grasses and other palatable herbs. The fragmentation of natural areas has meant that large mammals in search of good forage can no longer migrate across the biome to the same extent. They are now confined to reserves that have year-round forage – most of which are on the more fertile soils in the lowlands and in the mountains of the eastern part of the biome.

In fynbos, large mammalian predators require very large home ranges. In some cases their territories are larger than most conserved areas in the region.

For example, leopards (*Panthera pardus*) in the Stellenbosch area have home ranges of between 380 and 480 square kilometres – more than 10 times the average home range of leopards in African savannas.

This is a clear indication that food resources are limited in the region. Present low numbers of leopards and several other large mammals are dwindling even further because of habitat loss and other human-related factors.

Small mammals, on the other hand, are fairly common in fynbos, and many species have a marked influence on the way ecosystems

ABOVE The presence of restioids is a distinguishing feature that characterises fynbos.

CONSERVATION OF FYNBOS BIODIVERSITY

There are many good reasons for conserving fynbos biodiversity, ranging from the ethical and aesthetic arguments that rest on human values, through to the role that genetic diversity plays in evolution, and the practical consideration of potential uses for previously unexploited species. No-one knows what secrets the 526 Erica species, and the 245 species of Aspalathus hold. Maybe one species confined to a tiny 'island' of limestone on the Agulhas Plain will be the source of the wonder-drug of the 21st century?

*Some fynbos plants are currently of commercial importance. These include many species in the Proteaceae, Ericaceae, Bruniaceae and other families that are harvested from fynbos or cultivated for their attractive flowers. Thatching reed (*Thamnocortus erectus *and* T. insignis*), rooibos tea (*Aspalathus linearis*), honeybush tea (*Cyclopia spp.*), and several species of buchu (*Rutaceae family*) are others that have commercial uses. However, these 'useful' species form a tiny fraction of the total number of species. We must realise that intact fynbos communities provide the most important 'service' of all for humans by ensuring a reliable supply of clean water from mountain catchments. Apart from this vital function, fynbos also provides superb opportunities for recreation and is a huge drawcard for foreign tourism; an important economic consideration for South Africa's new democracy.*

ABOVE Male inflorescence of Thamnocortus *sp. – a type of restio.*

function. Their presence, abundance, and behaviour, like that of their larger cousins, are closely linked to the availability of food.

Striped mice (*Rhabdomys pumilio*), vlei rats (*Otomys irroratus*), Namaqua rock mice (*Aethomys namaquensis*) and other seed-feeders can have a profound effect on the plant communities. In the event of an untimely fire in spring, seeds of many *Protea* species are released from the canopy-held cones too early in the year. These seeds lie on the ground, vulnerable to seed feeders throughout the summer. With the start of the winter rains, none may be left to germinate. However, natural selection has favoured plants that protect their seeds against small mammals, and two prominent traits have evolved in the fynbos flora.

First, the seeds of many plants are dispersed and buried by ants, and second, many plants have canopy-held cones, which release their seeds only after scorching by fire, when fewer animals are around.

Fynbos does not host an unusual diversity of birds, and there are only six endemic species. The biome is not, however, without ornithological interest. Of the some 250 bird species that occur, many play significant ecological roles. For example, birds are important pollinators of many fynbos plants – they disperse the seeds of thicket and forest species – and are important regulators of insect and small mammal populations.

At higher altitudes, the striking Cape rockjumper (*Chaetops frenatus*) can be seen hopping from rock to rock on cliff faces, probing cracks for insects. Victorin's warbler (*Bradypterus victorini*), although secretive, is fairly common – the lively bubbling song of this 'fynbos special' is typical of the region.

The constant song of the Cape sugarbird (*Promerops cafer*), and the showy courtship behaviour of the male, who rises into the air above his territory and 'jerks' his body, flapping his long and impressive tail, are characteristic features of the Cape mountains during winter. The orange-breasted sunbird (*Nectarinia violacea*) is common at lower altitudes in winter when it feeds on the nectar of proteas and ericas, and in the summer, it is attracted to flowering ericas at higher altitudes. Sugarbirds and sunbirds are important pollinators of many proteas and ericas respectively.

Flocks of Cape siskin (*Serinus totta*) are often seen nesting and roosting in rock crevices, and foraging on buds, seeds and insects.

ABOVE A veld fire rages along the slopes of the Swartberg, darkening the sun with clouds of smoke.

ABOVE The progress of moist air from the ocean towards the interior is obstructed by steep mountain ranges that run parallel to the coastline.

Swartboskloof in the Jonkershoek Valley near Stellenbosch, is one of the best sites in the Western Cape to see protea canaries (*Serinus leucopterus*), and, indeed, the full range of fynbos birds. In a two-hour walk around this fascinating area one can see all six bird species that are endemic to the Cape Floristic Region. One reason for the relative scarcity of bird life in fynbos is that the vegetation has a relatively

uniform structure over much of the region. Compared with bushveld or forest, there is a small diversity of feeding opportunities, or niches, for birds. However, many of the most common birds in the fynbos biome are also found in the Karoo; this shows that they do not rely on any particular features of fynbos for their existence. There is usually relatively little change in the occurrence of bird species between

FYNBOS AND FIRE

*T*he word fire evokes many responses in the human psyche. It may be associated with warmth, comfort and feelings of well-being, but may also elicit emotions of fear and abhorrence. In nature, too, fire is both a destroyer and a regenerator of life.

Fire kills plants and animals, but also creates space and increases the availability of resources such as nutrients, light and water that otherwise limit regeneration in mature fynbos. Fire is a major mineralising agent, returning mineral elements held in living plants and litter to the soil. The flush of nutrients released after fire increases the availability of nitrogen, phosphorus and various chemical elements such as calcium and magnesium, enabling plants to re-establish in the nutrient-poor soils. These episodic flushes of nutrients are also crucial for many animals.

In response to recurring fires, natural selection led to the evolution of a host of special traits in fynbos plants. Fire stimulates seed release from cones held in the canopies of certain plants. It also stimulates seed germination, and even flowering in some plants. In some species, the heat of fire cracks the hard coat of seeds, facilitating the start of germination.

The dormant seeds of many fynbos species are stimulated to germinate by the chemical substances found in smoke. Similarly, substances leached from heated or charred wood can stimulate germination in some species. Many fynbos plants are, however, killed by fire, and rely entirely on seeds for reproduction. Others survive fires by resprouting from beneath fire-resistant bark or from below ground. The effect of fire on plant and animal communities in fynbos depends on many factors. These include the fire season, the intensity of the fire, and the time since the previous fire. Further influences are the amount of dry plant matter to act as fuel, and the weather conditions. Also important are the conditions that prevail just before and after fire – for example, the moisture content of the soil, and the abundance of animals that feed on seeds.

Natural fires can reoccur at intervals between four and 40 years, but the average cycle is about 15 years. Because fire is part of the functioning of fynbos ecosystems, it is essential for the long-term survival of fynbos. However, 'unnatural' fires, and fires that burn too frequently (less than the average cycle) or out of the natural summer/autumn season, are devastating, and can lead to species extinctions.

ABOVE *The rugged and dissected nature of the Cape landscape contributes considerably to the scenic beauty of the fynbos biome.*

adjacent landscapes, even if the composition of plant species is very different. Many bird species in fynbos are itinerant, roving the landscape in search of food. Migration may be predictable, as in the lesser double-collared sunbird (*Nectarinia chalybea*), which visits mountain areas in the southwestern parts of the biome only during summer and autumn, and especially between February and April, to feed on the nectar and insects in the flowers of several forest tree species. During the remainder of the year this bird lives in the lowlands where it breeds. Cape weavers (*Ploceus capensis*) are attracted to the lower mountain slopes by the abundant nectar and the insects associated with protea flowerheads between May and August.

Resident bird species in most fynbos areas occur at low densities and feed mainly on insects, or have a varied diet including insects, fruit, nectar and seeds.

Coastline

Roy A Lubke

South Africa's premier ecotoursim destination, and undoubtedly one of the country's finest assets, is

its 3 000-kilometre-long coastline. It is, in a very real sense, a major meeting point of man and nature.

Each year thousands of people flock from the hinterland to the coast. These people may revel in a leisurely

walk on an unspoilt shore, or snorkel, scuba dive, and marvel at the marine life, or even participate in a

myriad watersports. But what of the nature, ecology and conservation of South Africa's coastline?

How many visitors to the sunny shores of South Africa consider these issues as they bask in the

sun and bathe in the waters of this magnificent coast?

nterestingly, South Africa's coastline is not particularly long when compared with countries that have dissected coastlines and offshore islands, such as Greece. Nevertheless, it diplays great variations along its range – both in the shape of the land as it meets the sea, and in the marine life that lives along it. Many agents induce these variations, the most influential, of course, being the ocean currents that sweep down the east coast and up the west coast. The Mozambique Current makes the sea warm and subtropical along the east coast. This current aids evaporation, resulting in generally high rainfall and lush vegetation on the land. In stark contrast, the Benguela Current has its origins in Antarctic waters – hence a cold sea along the west coast. Cold water resists evaporation, and also causes condensation of moisture carried by breezes from warmer

parts of the Atlantic Ocean before it can reach the western shores of South Africa. The result is a generally arid terrestrial environment on the west coast. Especially along the Cape coast, the marine climate is particularly severe and features strong winds and storms.

These forces have chiselled away at the geology of the land, forming numerous coves, bays and rocky headlands.

Currents, tides and wave action all play a role in the continual shaping of the shoreline. On one hand, the land may be eroded away, but on the other, it may also be expanded, by the depositing of sand. Regions with lower rainfall along parts of the south and southeast coast, often support vast dune systems. Here sand is brought ashore by the currents, accumulates on the beaches and is shaped by the wind into dunes.

LEFT A Cape cormorant clings to the rock cliffs and contemplates a dive into the turbulent waters off Cape Point in search of another meal.
ABOVE Wave after wave invade the sandy shores of Goukamma Nature Reserve.

The Alexandria dune field on the northern shore of Algoa Bay is one of the largest coastal dune fields in the world, stretching some 50 kilometres from the Sundays River to Woody Cape. High dunes also occur further up the east coast and toward KwaZulu-Natal, but these are covered in vegetation. This happens because the rainfall is higher and plants have managed to take hold, thereby stabilising the dune systems. By contrast, the extensive dune fields of the West Coast are bare.

COASTLINE REGIONS
The coast can be divided into six regions.

West Coast
Stretching from the mouth of the Orange River, which forms the border with Namibia, southwards to the mouth of the Olifants River at Papendorp, is the West Coast. It is characteristically dry strandveld – an arid shrub-land – with a low, winter rainfall.

Southwest coast
The Southwest coast stretches from the Olifants River to Cape Agulhas. It is a winter-rainfall region and the terrestrial vegetation type is fynbos.

South coast
The south coast, stretching from Cape Agulhas to Cape St Francis, where the rainfall, as one progresses eastwards, moves from a winter to seasonal spring or summer regime. The vegetation types include dune fynbos and a mosaic of thicket and forest in some high rainfall areas.

ABOVE A colony of Cape gannets is an incredible visual spectacle. It is also an onslaught on the other senses: the colony is also extremely noisy and smelly! This misty scene is set on Bird Island at Lambert's Bay.

ABOVE Hanging in the breeze, a Hartlaub's gull shows off its perfect design for graceful flight. These gulls forage on the coasts and islands of the western Cape and Namibia, and are vagrants to the east coast.

Southeast coast

This coast, from Cape St Francis to Kei Mouth, has dune fynbos in the west and dune thicket and coastal grasslands in the eastern regions. Here the rainfall is variable, falling in either spring and autumn, or in summer.

Wild Coast

Extending northwards from Kei Mouth to Umtamvuna River the Wild Coast consists mainly of coastal grassland on steep and rocky shores, with dune thicket or forest in the kloofs and valleys. Rainfall occurs in the summer.

KwaZulu-Natal coast

Stretching from the Umtamvuna River to Mozambique, this narrow, summer-rainfall coastline area is covered with dune thicket or coastal forest.

ECOLOGY: MARINE LIFE AND HABITATS

The many coastal environments include marine or rocky shores, where there is a multitude of intertidal animals and seaweeds; the estuarine environments, where the rivers open to the sea; sandy beaches and dunes either mobile or stabilised by vegetation; and rocky shores or cliffs that are often wave-splashed and so have a low vegetation cover.

Marine life forms of South African coastal waters can be classified into three categories. The first of these is plankton – a collection of plant and animal organisms that passively drift or float on the water and are sometimes microscopic in size. The second group includes the actively swimming animals – known as nekton – found in all waters, and include microscopic animals as well as free-swimming fish. The third category

CONSERVATION

Unfortunately, along our long and beautiful coast there is very little that has been left undisturbed.

On the west coast, the West Coast National Park in the Saldanha-Langebaan region conserves the estuarine system and the strandveld vegetation. On the southern coast, the largest conservation region is the Tsitsikamma National Park, which is an area of rocky shore with fynbos and forest in the kloofs and gulleys leading inland. The Wilderness Lakes area is semi-protected, but not conserved as a true wilderness area. Many smaller parks occur along the Cape coast, and in the Transkei.

KwaZulu-Natal has an active conservation policy, but there are limited areas for conservation except along the Maputaland coast in the north, which includes conserved areas such as Kosi Bay and Sodwana Bay, and the Greater St Lucia Wetland Park.

The South African coastline is an important asset for tourism. Appropriate design and planning along our coastline can bring about the conservation of many of the attractive areas, as well as the sustainable use of the region for tourism. Holiday resorts must be appropriately planned and development should be confined to certain places. Increasing research on the conservation of the marine resources will lead to a better understanding of how these can be utilised in a sustainable way. For example many different species of seaweeds are not sustainably utilised to their full extent, as they are in the Far Eastern countries.

Although some areas of the coastline have already been over-exploited, with sensible planning and appropriate development it can be made more widely accessible to tourists, and still maintain its character.

is the benthos group, which consists of bottom-dwelling, creeping and crawling animals and sedentary plants (seaweeds). All three categories occur within the following coastal habitats.

Rocky shores and headlands

Along the rocky shores and where cliffs drop into the sea, there is very often little sand and, with high winds and tides and wave action, spray is thrown onto the cliffs. This makes for a very harsh environment, and the plants and animals living here must be able to withstand the high salinity of the sea water and the salt-laden winds. Grasslands often grow above these rocky shores, therefore, as the larger woody plants are unable to establish themselves.

The intertidal zone along rocky shores is one of the most stressful habitats for plants and animals. As the tide rises and falls twice daily, the organisms living here are constantly buffeted by wave action and are exposed to air during the low tides, as well as to wind, sun and high temperature, especially during the summer months. Thus these plants and animals are specially adapted to withstand the constant changes of this very variable environment.

They are found in many different forms and varieties. If one explores a rocky shore at low tide, it will be apparent that its inhabitants occur in distinct zonation patterns as one moves from the higher tide levels to the low tide level. These zonations vary according to the type of rock substrates and also the temperature of the water. Generally there is an upper zone dominated by periwinkles, followed by one of barnacles. In the lowest intertidal zone, limpets are predominant, and at subtidal level, many different seaweeds occur.

Sandy beaches and dunes

Dune fields are always changing, as more and more sand accumulates from the sea and is blown ashore. Although they may also appear to be barren wastes, they provide a number of habitats for a diversity of plant

ABOVE   Kranshoek in the southern Cape. Here the rocks form the habitat of many intertidal life forms.

and animal life. Some plant species are pioneers, colonising mobile sands. Other species are found in more sheltered dune slacks or hollows, and yet others in complex bush pockets or dune thicket, where a more stable plant community has already been established.

The pioneer plant species have to be able to withstand the harsh conditions of extreme high and low temperatures, variable water supply, strong winds, accumulating sand and salt spray. The pioneer species can often tolerate flooding by sea water, and the seeds may be dispersed in the sea, or by wind or mechanical means to other uninhabited sandy environments. Usually the seedlings will germinate in small hollows along the driftline where organic matter accumulates. Once they become established, they will help to trap the sand, and the dune will grow as small hammocks (or ridges) form around the plants. As plants become well established, various new animal and plant species move in.

All the while, sand is building up, and it is in this way that massive dunes such as those along the KwaZulu-Natal coast have grown to vast proportions. The highest plant-covered dunes in the world occur in this region, near Mapelane. These dunes are covered with tall forests and communities of a variety of different plant and animal species.

Although the presence of life forms on a sandy beach might not be immediately evident, plant and animal species are indeed there – albeit buried in the sand.

And while there may be relatively few species, they will emerge to feed when covered by water.

In addition, there are millions of floating microscopic algae (phytoplankton) in the waters, which are the main food of filter feeders such as sand mussels and clams that live in the sand. The zooplankton – that is, floating animal life also – feed on these algae. In turn, members of the higher groups such as the fishes feed on the zooplankton.

In some areas where the phytoplankton forms golden brown patches or blooms in the surf, some fishes, such as mullet, will feed directly on the millions of small plants.

ABOVE North of Yzerfontein, a beach in the West Coast National Park is shrouded in clammy mist rolling in from the icy Atlantic Ocean. The shores of the West Coast are often littered with shells of sand mussels.

ABOVE The Cape cormorant is the most abundant sea bird breeding on the islands off the South African and Namibian coasts.

Kelp beds

Dense beds of kelp are a conspicuous feature of the southwest and west coasts of South Africa. These underwater 'forests', which may extend some three kilometres offshore, create ideal living conditions for a multitude of marine life. Not only do they provide a major source of food for animals, but they also break the force of the waves and thus provide shelter for animals and other plants. Kelp beds are commercially very important as they provide a habitat for the rock lobsters (crayfish) that support an important sea-fishing industry.

Estuaries

Estuaries are the meeting places of rivers and the salt waters of the sea, and their character depends on the amount of fresh water in the river, and also on the form of the land. Some estuaries are continuously open, but many South African estuaries are closed by sandbars except during the rainy season.

Along the southeast coast there are a number of large estuaries and some very beautiful, unspoilt ones such as Mngazana on the Transkei coast. The KwaZulu-Natal coast has large estuarine systems, although some are disturbed and have been completely altered by harbours, such as at Durban Bay and Richards Bay. The largest estuarine system in South Africa is Lake St Lucia, with an area of some 300 square kilometres. Some estuarine systems, notably Lake St Lucia and, on the west coast, the Saldanha-Langebaan system, are wetlands of international importance (see 'Rivers and Wetlands', pages 52–63). The estuaries that are open to the sea shores, which may become extremely saline by evaporation, have extensive salt marshes. Here one encounters plants able to grow in the silty, muddy soil. Like the intertidal rocky shores, these marshes are divided into easily identifiable zones as the tide rises and falls. The plant communities form the zones here and are habitats for many different types of invertebrate animals such as mud prawns and crabs. This is also an important breeding ground for fish. Within the estuary itself, at subtidal level, there may be a number of seagrasses, although only eel grass is found in the Cape waters. In more subtropical systems, there are a number of other seagrass species. Also character-istic of the warmer waters of the east coast are the mangrove systems. These include a number of species of trees which are able to tolerate the saline conditions and help to stabilize the muddy banks of estuaries.

BIRD LIFE

The South African coastline is blessed with a rich variety of bird species. Some of them are rare and endangered, others are extremely abundant.

The jackass penguin (*Spheniscus demersus*) is endemic to the southern African coastline, and it is the only penguin that breeds on the African continent. Its name refers to its donkey-like, braying call. Large numbers of the population have been lost in modern times, mainly to oil pollution and the reduction of their food resource by commercial overfishing.

The Cape cormorant (*Phalacrocorax capensis*) is one of the most abundant fish-eating birds breeding on South Africa's offshore islands. The Cape gannet (*Morus capensis*) is a beautiful, gregarious sea bird. As a breeding species, it is endemic to the southern African coastline. It is mostly seen along the west coast, but it follows the sardine runs up the KwaZulu-Natal coast during the winter months and may move as far afield as Kenya on the east coast and the Spanish Sahara on the west coast in its search for food.

Hartlaub's gull (*Larus hartlaubii*), another graceful southern African endemic, is an opportunistic scavenger and is often found in and around the more developed areas of the coast, where it finds rich pickings.

Cormorants, gannets and penguins breed on tiny islands off the shores of the Western and Eastern Cape, and Namibia.

In the breeding season these colonies are among the most dramatic ornithological spectacles a bird-watcher could hope to see. The colonies are overcrowded, smelly and noisy, but the interactions of the birds, whether affectionate or hostile, will keep most birders engrossed for hours.

African black oystercatchers (*Haematopus moquini*) too are endemic to the southern African coastline. Its beak is laterally flattened – an adaptation to prise oysters and mussels loose from their rocky habitat.

ABOVE The sun rises over tranquil waters of the Indian Ocean.

ABOVE Lichens colonise a rock surface in the Robberg Nature Reserve.

ABOVE Carpobrotus *is a pioneer plant colonising sandy beaches. Members of this genus release chemical substances that inhibit the growth of competitive plants.*

The Road Ahead

John Hanks

In 1872, the first national park in the world was created at Yellowstone in the USA. Since then, a mosaic of 8 641 designated protected areas that meet internationally accepted IUCN – The World Conservation Union's criteria have been set up by governments around the world. In 1895, the first official South African game reserve – Hluhluwe – was established in what was then Natal.

South Africa now has 388 areas under the protection of government conservation agencies, covering 6 529 369 hectares, or 5.8 per cent of the country's surface. A further 889 areas, comprising 333 037 hectares of private land are subject to conservation management in one form or another.

PEOPLE AND CONSERVATION

South Africa has every reason to be proud of its protected area network, but in common with all other nations, these protected areas are coming under direct and indirect threat as a consequence of the accelerating pace of global change. Each year, from now until well into the 21st century, 90 million people will be added to the world total.

In sub-Saharan Africa, unlike in most other parts of the world, fertility decline has only just begun to appear. The region's fertility rate stood at 6.7 in 1960, and was still at 6.2 in 1995. (By definition, the fertility rate is the number of births per 1 000 women in the 15–44 age group.)

Nobody can dispute that Africa's high population growth rate will heighten demands for food, water, energy, housing, employment, education and medical services. But can these demands be met within the economic constraints the continent is facing, and will they be met without inflicting irreparable environmental damage?

With these rapidly growing human populations comes quickening land transformation, with the continent's forests, woodlands, grasslands, soil and estuaries caught up in an intensifying spiral of degradation, with a cascading series of environmental catastrophes, which in turn have seriously depleted and degraded surface and ground water sources, and exacerbated the scale of human suffering. Concomitantly, there has been an increase of the impact of pollutants on the environment, and a change in climate patterns. Unfortunately, Africa's protected areas, and South Africa is no exception, are not immune to these changes.

Derogation of protected areas is increasing, with human encroachment and the illegal harvesting of fauna and flora threatening to destroy the territorial and ecological integrity of the national parks and game reserves. An additional threat has come from those who question the value of protected areas. Often the questioning is ill-informed, based on the perception that protected areas are nothing more than sanctuaries set aside for the enjoyment of a privileged elite.

Against the background of Africa's daunting scenario of socio-economic and environmental problems, it is perfectly understandable that these sanctuaries should be regarded as anachronisms in a continent where so many have so little.

IUCN's Jeffrey McNeely has succinctly addressed the 'perception threat' by listing six reasons why protected areas should be recognised and accepted as being of crucial and growing national importance.

McNeely argues that protected areas: (1) safeguard many of the world's outstanding areas of living richness, natural beauty and cultural significance, are a source of inspiration and are an irreplaceable asset of the countries to which they belong; (2) help to maintain the diversity of ecosystems, species, genetic varieties and ecological processes (including the regulation of water flow and climate), which are vital for the support of all life on earth and for the improvement of human social and economic conditions; (3) protect genetic varieties and species that are vital in meeting human needs, for example in agriculture and medicine, and are the basis for human social and cultural adaptation in an uncertain and changing world; (4) often are home to communities of people with traditional cultures and an irreplaceable knowledge of nature; (5) have significant scientific, educational, cultural, recreational and spiritual value; and (6) provide major direct and indirect benefits to local and national economies.

If these arguments are not sufficient to dissuade those who would like to see some of South Africa's protected areas degazetted and opened up for grazing and human settlement, then an equally compelling argument is that the 'conservation option' is very often the best and most sustainable form of land use, both ecologically and economically.

The recently created 75 000 ha Madikwe Game Reserve in the North-West Province is a good example. This new reserve will generate 1 200 jobs at a minimum wage of R700 per month, and neighbouring communities will earn a percentage of entrance fees and hunting rights. Consumptive use of wildlife is an integral part of this new development. Had the land been allocated to cattle farmers, only 80 jobs (at between R50 and R150 per month) would have been created, with the inevitable overcrowding and overgrazing following not far behind.

BIODIVERSITY

Environmental conservation does not stop at the boundaries of designated protected areas, and it is regrettable that far too few South Africans, particularly politicians, have grasped this vitally important precept. As part of the road ahead to the creation of this awareness, an essential first step is to give an economic value to the environment based on the importance of conserving biodiversity.

The word 'biodiversity', a contraction of biological diversity, describes and encapsulates the variety and variability of life on earth. Biodiversity is usually defined at three levels: genetic diversity – the variation between individuals and between populations within a species;

ABOVE *The strangely shaped hamerkop is a common South African waterbird. In tribal folklore it is sometimes regarded as a harbinger of bad luck.*

ABOVE *Spot-lit cliffs in the Golden Gate Highlands National Park, in the Free State.*

species diversity – the different types of plants, animals and other life forms within a region; and community or ecosystem diversity – the variety of habitats found within an area.

It is difficult to grasp the scale of the diversity involved. Taking species diversity alone, without looking at genetic variation within species, some 1.7 million species of organisms have been described by taxonomists, and Professor EO Wilson recently estimated that there are probably another 100 million species worldwide waiting to be described and catalogued, most of these being insects and microorganisms. Numbers alone can never do justice to form and function, to colour and camouflage, to nature's inspired striving to survive and reproduce in an often hostile world. For the record, South Africa has one of the highest biodiversity indices in the world, exceeded only by those of Brazil and Indonesia. We have the richest flora of all the African countries, with over 20 300 species of plants. There are 227 species of mammals, more than 700 species of birds, 103 species of snakes, and 630 species of butterflies. In the 400 square kilometres of the Cape Peninsula Protected Natural Environment alone, there are no less than 2 856 species of plants (the whole of the British Isles has a mere 1 492 species), and 157 of these are endemic, occurring nowhere else on earth.

How do we go about giving an economic value to this extraordinary celebration of biodiversity? It can be done by attaching an economic value to each of the three levels of biodiversity, all three of which have direct and indirect benefits and values.

Genetic diversity

Genetic diversity represents the heritable variation within and between populations of organisms.

ABOVE *Sociable Burchell's zebra drink at a seasonal water pan in lush summer veld.*

New genetic variation arises in individuals by gene and chromosome mutations, and in organisms with sexual reproduction, this can be spread through the population by recombination. To put that variation into perspective, it has been estimated that in both humans and fruit flies, the number of possible combinations of different forms of each gene sequence exceeds the number of atoms in the universe. However, only a small fraction (often less than one per cent) of the genetic material of higher organisms is outwardly expressed in the form and function of the organism.

This genetic diversity, which is inherent in species, provides the raw material to respond rapidly to changing circumstances, although these responses may not always be in our interest, such as when animal pathogens or agricultural pests develop resistance to our control measures.

The economic value of this variation is well illustrated by considering where our food comes from. Over 90 per cent of our food depends upon a mere 20 plant species and 10 animal species, most of which were first used by our ancestors in the Stone Age. They learned initially how to domesticate the more productive forms of wild plants, using selective breeding to meet our requirements.

Nearly all the staple foods of today, including most of our cereals, root crops and several legumes, were first cultivated during the Stone Age, but in the process of selection, there was a narrowing of the original genetic base of the wild species, which means that there has been a loss of genetic determinants controlling such things as disease resistance and adaptation to different environments. Increasingly, plant and animal breeders are depending upon genetic material from wild relatives in order to introduce pest and disease resistance. Related species can also

provide genetic material to improve nutritional quality and durability. In fact, the use of nature's genetic diversity has the potential to save farmers millions of rands each year, at the same time as increasing productivity. The wild relatives are often obscure, little-known species, and with South Africa's high biodiversity index, genetic material of inestimable value must be there waiting to be used.

Species diversity

The arguments for the economic value of species diversity are equally as compelling.

Species diversity provides humankind with an astonishing variety of plants and animals and their products for use as food, medicines, fuel, cosmetics, industrial products and building materials, and some of these species have even inspired industrial design. For example, the earth contains at least 75 000 edible plants, but of these only about 150 have been cultivated on a large scale.

The potential number of new foods that could be developed from wild plants is clearly immense. New fruits and vegetables are already making their way into markets.

The fynbos biome has excellent examples of species of economic value, as illustrated by the many internationally familiar horticultural subjects that originated from the fynbos, and have been bred and hybridised throughout the world. They include gladioli, freesias, and pelargoniums (geraniums). More recently horticulturalists have made extensive use of nemesias, vygies, several daisies, proteas and a number of bulbous groups such as ixias and sparaxis. Proteas and ericas are much in demand overseas, and millions of rands in foreign exchange are generated each year from these sales. Fynbos has also yielded several medicinal/quasi medicinal plants such as rooibos tea and buchu, with

ABOVE Anacampseros papyracea *mimics the quartz pebbles among which it grows.*

THE IUCN

Founded in 1948, IUCN – The World Conservation Union, brings together states, government agencies, and a diverse range of non-governmental organisations (NGOs) in a unique membership: 880 members in all, spread across 133 countries. The Union builds its strengths from its members, networks and partners to enhance its capacity to support global alliances to safeguard natural resources at local, regional and global levels. IUCN's Commission on National Parks and Protected Areas (CNPPA) is specifically responsible for promoting the establishment of a worldwide network of effectively managed terrestrial and marine protected, areas and has distributed guidelines on this topic, including an international system of categories.

ABOVE Early morning mist adds a touch of delicacy to a savanna scene with contorted trees and autumn grass.

dozens of other species being widely used for traditional healing. With the high species diversity within the fynbos biome, it is reasonable to expect that there are many more useful species waiting to be discovered.

On the animal side, the potential for using Africa's extraordinary faunal diversity is equally great. In Botswana, over 50 species of wild animals provide animal protein exceeding 90 kilograms per person per year. Over three million kilograms of meat is obtained from the springhare alone. In the Kalahari, the Bushmen enjoy cockroaches (among other insects). In South Africa there is a great potential for rearing insects for both direct human consumption, and for feeding to chickens and pigs. For example, swarming termites are readily taken as food by man and eaten raw. They contain 46 per cent protein and 44 per cent fat – better than a sirloin steak, which offers only 23 per cent protein and 32 per cent fat. Freshwater fish are equally important as a source of protein in poor rural areas. In Maputaland, a traditional *fonya* fishing drive by 500 people, lasting no more than three hours, may yield up to three tons of fish.

There is no doubt that new food sources (naturally adapted to difficult climate and soil conditions) and new medicinal plants will have a meaningful role to play in improving the health and living standards of human populations throughout Africa, an economic value of growing importance as more people move onto the continent's marginal lands.

Community or ecosystem diversity

Community or ecosystem diversity is the last of the three levels of biodiversity, and in terms of economic value, perhaps the most important and least appreciated. Far too few people recognise the essential role of plants, animals and microorganisms in our ecosystem services or life-support systems, an example being the role of natural forests, grasslands and wetlands in our water catchment. These areas consist

of an intricate complex of plant and animal species (including key organisms involved in soil formation) that interact to their mutual advantages. Catchments help to absorb, store and regulate the flow of water. When these areas are destroyed, there is a general lowering of the water table, with springs and rivers drying up, and water quality declining, accelerating the spread of water-borne diseases, and reducing peoples' productivity. Throughout Africa this is accompanied by an increase in siltation of rivers, and flash floods across agricultural land downstream, eventually destroying the estuaries and the species associated with them. These impacts have a multi-million rand price-tag associated with them.

ABOVE A drowsy lion and his mate savour the early morning sunlight.

ABOVE Langebaan Lagoon, on the Cape's West Coast.

With the destruction of biodiversity, soil genesis is impeded, nutrients are not recycled efficiently, the atmosphere is not cleaned and the carbon and nitrogen cycles are adversely affected. We must recognise that even if this loss of biodiversity and degradation of the environment does not reach life-threatening levels, it can result in a major decline in the quality of life of the world in which we live.

A combination of species and ecosystem diversity forms the basis of Africa's tourism industry, one of the continent's biggest earners of foreign currency, and a major employer. South Africa's travel and tourism economy alone was worth R53.2 billion in 1998, and employed 737 600 people. South Africa is building up a deserved international reputation for the quality of its magnificent mosaic of designated protected wildlife sanctuaries, drawcards of an industry that has an enormous growth potential. The maintenance of the territorial integrity of these national parks and game reserves, and the provision of adequate resources and staff for their management, makes good economic sense by any standards.

Finally, at the bottom of the economic scale of the value of biodiversity, is the broad grouping of 'non-use' values, such as the role of natural areas for their intrinsic aesthetic values, for inspiration for paintings, sculptures, music, literature, poetry and for human spiritual upliftment.

Trying to look at the value of environmental conservation through the eyes of an economist is a difficult approach, but it is worth pursuing. We have much to learn on the empirical application of realistic economic values, although ethicists might argue that it is wrong even to attempt such an exercise because you cannot quantify 'quality of life'. These are subjective value judgements, which have radically different cultural interpretations, particularly here in Africa. However, these difficulties should not be an excuse for inaction.

CONSERVATION AND DEVELOPMENT RELATIONSHIPS

In 1991, the United Nations Environmental Programme (UNEP), IUCN and the World Wide Fund for Nature (WWF) published *Caring for the Earth – A Strategy for Sustainable Living*.

This seminal publication has been instrumental in stimulating some new thinking on the relationship between conservation and development, and between conservation and people, encapsulated in the following quote: 'Development must be people-centred, but it must be conservation-based.'

Campaigns of passion and idealism will not halt the loss of Africa's biodiversity, for they have no relevance to those who live in poverty.

The challenge facing the continent lies in finding appropriate forms of development that will break the vicious cycle of poverty, population growth and renewable resource depletion, and reduce the continent's rapidly increasing environmental debt. Conservation programmes that stress the economic value of biodiversity will stand a much better chance of being accepted by disadvantaged communities who all too often regard 'conservation' as meaning 'hands off, keep out'. A pragmatic approach of this nature would view environmental and developmental goals as being inextricably linked. It would not sacrifice the territorial and ecological integrity of designated protected areas, which is, as always, a concern to 'traditional' conservationists.

Environmental neglect inevitably leads to economic and social collapse. 'Conservation with people' backed up by strong economic arguments should not only help to reverse environmental neglect, and give a real purpose to the maintenance of protected areas, but it will also restore human dignity and self-respect. The choice is ours.

ABOVE The Lowveld is particularly beautiful in summer, when the vegetation is a verdant green and the bush is alive with baby impalas.

Contributors

GEORGE J BREDENKAMP is a professor of plant ecology and a specialist on grassland and bushveld vegetation, with a special interest in the application of ecology in agriculture, nature conservation, horticulture and landscape architecture. He has acted as ecological consultant on more than 100 ecology-related projects.

NOEL VAN ROOYEN is associate professor of plant ecology at the University of Pretoria. He is a savanna ecologist with a special interest in veld utilisation by game, and the management of nature reserves and game ranches. He is a member of six national and international professional botanical and ecological societies, and has authored or co-authored more than 77 scientific and popular articles, and 43 scientific reports.

DANNY WALMSLEY is an environmental scientist, with wide experience in all fields of environmental management. Dr Walmsley has a PhD in aquatic science and over 25 years' experience in the management of freshwater ecosystems. He has been involved in research programmes on most of South Africa's major river systems, reservoirs and wetland areas, and currently runs his own environmental and management consulting business in Pretoria.

JAY WALMSLEY is an environment scientist, with 10 years' experience in aquatic ecology, including policy development and management of aquatic systems. She has an MSc in aquatic zoology from the University of Cape Town, and her main interests lie in water resource management using economic instruments, resource information management and resource sustainability. She currently works in Pretoria as an environmental and management consultant.

WAYNE MATTHEWS is employed as a senior research scientist by the KwaZulu-Natal Nature Conservation Service. As a plant ecologist he has conducted intensive research on the vegetation of the Escarpment. His research at the Blyde River Canyon brought to light the flowering plant *Haemanthus pauculifolius*, until then unknown. Wayne is currently finalising his PhD on the vegetation of Maputaland.

JUNE WENDY LLOYD is a senior researcher in the field of remote sensing for the Agricultural Research Council's Institute for Soil, Climate and Water. Ms Lloyd's special fields of interest include the functioning and dynamics of arid and semiarid ecosystems, and the application of remote sensing and geographic information systems (GIS) technology in conservation planning, management and monitoring, and in the mapping and monitoring of alien plant infestations.

ANNELISE LE ROUX is employed in scientific services at Cape Nature Conservation and is currently involved in conservation planning in the Western Cape Province. Her love for arid regions and, in particular, the succulent karoo, has evolved through 25 years of research on Namaqualand vegetation and flora. Ms Le Roux has been involved with the series of *South African Wild Flower Guides* – published by the Botanical Society of South Africa – as editor and Afrikaans translator, and is also the author of one of the titles in this series.

DR GRETEL VAN ROOYEN is a lecturer and senior research officer in the Department of Botany at the University of Pretoria. Her main research interest focuses on the ephemeral plants of Namaqualand, with special emphasis on their population dynamics and adaptations to their unpredictable environment. Dr Van Rooyen is currently writing a book on wild flowers of the Cederberg, Clanwilliam and the Biedouw Valley, in the series *South African Wild Flower Guides*.

ROY ALLEN LUBKE is an associate professor of botany at Rhodes University. He has a PhD in grass taxonomy from the University of Western Ontario, and, together with two colleagues, he established the Coastal and Environmental Services in 1989. Professor Lubke has, through involvement in environmental impact assessments in East Africa and Mozambique, studied the ecology of these regions and recently described coastal forests of Mozambique dominated by a previously undescribed tree species. His current research activities include restoration and dune ecology, and studies on the local vegetation of the Eastern Cape.

DR COERT J GELDENHUYS has worked as a forestry scientist with the Department of Forestry at Saasveld, George, and at the CSIR (Environmentek) in Pretoria. In 1997, he set up his own small company, ForestWood cc, to continue his work as a consulting forest ecologist. His particular interest lies in the development of sustainable, integrated, multiple resource use systems in forest and woodland, including ecotourism and forest restoration. He has collected new plant species, including a small tree named *Apodytes geldenhuysii*.

DR DAVE RICHARDSON is chief research officer and deputy director at the Institute for Plant Conservation, at the University of Cape Town. His research focuses on the ecology of alien plant invasions and other conservation issues in the Cape Floristic Region. He is co-author of the best-selling book *Fynbos – South Africa's Unique Foral Kingdom* (Fernwood Press, 1995). Dr Richardson serves on the IUCN – The World Conservation Union's Species Survival Specialist Group on Invasive Organisms.

DR JOHN HANKS (MA.PhD.Cantab) has worked in conservation all over southern Africa, firstly in Kafue and Luangwa national parks, Zambia, and then with the University of Rhodesia. In 1975, he was appointed chief professional officer of the Natal Parks Board, South Africa, and in 1978 became professor and head of the Department of Biological Sciences at Natal University, and first director of the Institute of Natural Resources. After 12 years with the WWF, initially in Switzerland as director of the Africa Programme, and then as chief executive, WWF – South Africa, Dr Hanks was invited in 1997 to head the Peace Parks Foundation, newly formed to facilitate the establishment of transfrontier conservation areas across Africa.

George Bredenkamp, Noel van Rooyen and Roy Lubke have all contributed to the widely acclaimed *Vegetation of South Africa, Lesotho and Swaziland* (Department of Environmental Affairs & Tourism, 1996).

Bibliography & Further Reading

Africa – A Natural History. Stuart, Chris & Tilde. (Southern Book Publishers, 1995.)

Africa's Vanishing Wildlife. Stuart, Chris & Tilde. (Southern Book Publishers, 1996.)

African Insect Life. Skaife, SH; Ledger, John and Bannister, Anthony. (Struik, 1979.)

Aspects of Life – A Natural History of Southern Africa. Chambers, Richard and Odendall, Francois. (Struik, 1996.)

Atlas of Southern African Birds, The. Harrison, JA; Allan, DG; Underhill, LG; Herremans, M; Tree, AJ; Parker, V and Brown, CJ (Eds). (Birdlife South Africa, 1997.)

Biomes of Southern Africa – An Objective Categorization. Rutherford, MC and Westfall RH. (Memoirs of the Botanical Survey of South Africa 54: 1-98, 1986.)

Biotic Diversity in Southern Africa. Huntley, BJ (Ed.). (Oxford University Press Cape Town, 1989.)

Bushveld Trees – Lifeblood of the Transvaal Lowveld. Borchert, Peter; Van Wyk, Braam and Funston, Malcolm. (Fernwood Press, 1993.)

Cape Floral Kingdom, The. Paterson-Jones, Colin. (New Holland, 1997.)

Complete Book of Southern African Birds, The. Ginn, PJ; McIlleron, WG; Milstein, P Le S. (Struik Winchester, 1996.)

Complete Book of Southern African Mammals, The. Mills, Gus and Hes, Lex. (Struik Winchester, 1997.)

Complete Guide to the Freshwater Fishes of Southern Africa, A. Skelton, Paul. (Southern Book Publishers, 1993.)

Crowded Desert, The – The Kalahari Gemsbok National Park. Nussey, Wilf. (William Waterman Publications, 1993.)

Exploring the Natural Wonders of South Africa. Olivier, Willie and Sandra. (Struik Publishers, 1996.)

Fynbos – South Africa's Unique Floral Kingdom. Cowling, Richard; Richardson, Dave and Paterson-Jones, Colin. (Fernwood Press, 1995.)

Game Parks & Nature Reserves of Southern Africa. (Reader's Digest Association, South Africa, 1997.)

Genus Conophytum, The. Hammer, Steven. (Succulent Plant Publications, 1993.)

Guide to Southern African Game & Nature Reserves. Stuart, Chris and Tilde. (Struik Publishers, 1997.)

Guide to the Grasses of Southern Africa. Van Oudtshoorn, Frits. (Briza Publications, 1999.)

Guide to the Kalahari Gemsbok National Park. Mills, Gus and Haagner, Clem. (Southern Book Publishers, 1989.)

Kalahari, The – Survival in a Thirstland Wilderness. Dennis, Nigel J; Knight, Michael and Joyce, Peter. (Struik Publishers, 1997.)

Kruger Park, The – Wonders of an African Eden. Dennis, Nigel J and Scholes, Bob. (New Holland Publishers, 1995.)

Living Deserts of Southern Africa, The. Lovegrove, Barry. (Fernwood Press, 1993)

Living Shores of Southern Africa, The. Branch, Margo & George and Bannister, Anthony. (Struik Publishers, 1998.)

Making the most of Indigenous Trees. Venter, Fanie & Julye-Ann. (Briza Publications, 1996.)

Mammals of the Southern African Subregion, The. Skinner, JD and Smithers, RHN. (University of Pretoria, 1990.)

Mammals of the Southern African Subregion. Smithers, RHN. (University of Pretoria, 1983.)

Reptiles of Southern Africa. Patterson, Rod and Bannister, Anthony. (Struik Publishers, 1987.)

Roberts' Birds of Southern Africa. Maclean, Gordon Lindsay. (John Voelcker Bird Book Fund, 1998.)

Safari Companion, The. Estes, Richard D. (Russel Friedman Books, 1993.)

Sasol Birds of Prey of Africa and its Islands. Kemp, Alan & Meg. (New Holland Publishers, 1998.)

Sasol Proteas: A Field Guide to the Proteas of Southern Africa. Rebelo, Tony. (Fernwood Press, 1995.)

Scenic South Africa. Fraser, Sean. (Sunbird Publishers, 1998.)

Smiths' Sea Fishes. Smith, Margaret M and Heemstra, Phillip C (Eds). (Southern Book Publishers, 1995.)

Trees of Southern Africa. Coates Palgrave, Keith. (Struik Publishers, 1983.)

Two Oceans – Guide to the marine life of Southern Africa. Branch, GM; Griffiths, CL; Branch, ML and Beckley, LE. (David Philips, 1994.)

Vegetation of South Africa, Lesotho and Swaziland. Low, AB and Rebelo, AG (Eds). (Department of Environmental Affairs & Tourism, 1996.)

Veld types of South Africa. Acocks, JPH. (Memoirs of the Botanical Survey of South Africa 57:1-146, 1988, 1st ed. 1953.)

Wild South Africa. Hes, Lex and Mountain, Alan. (Struik Publishers, 1998.)

Wild Ways: A Field Guide to Mammal Behaviour in South Africa. Apps, Peter. (Southern Book Publishers, 1992.)

Index